Praise for
Completely His
lead book in the Loving Jesus Without Limits series

"Engaging and soulful."
—PUBLISHER'S WEEKLY

"Shannon Ethridge's life exhibits God's transforming power. Her response to tragedy will guide others who struggle through dark valleys, to find the light of hope that is in Christ."
—MAX LUCADO, best-selling author

"When the worst has happened, only time can bring perspective and turn trauma into triumph. Shannon Ethridge is an incredible woman who has a story to tell and a passion to share. Through experiences that would level most, she has risen as a lover of Jesus who can speak to the heart of every woman. *Completely His* calls even the most timid or scarred to a place of deep, sweet relationship with the One who patiently waits for His beloved to lean in and trust Him. I loved the book. I love Shannon's heart."
—JAN SILVIOUS, author of *Foolproofing Your Life*
and *Big Girls Don't Whine*

"Insightful and daring, *Completely His* so challenged me to look at myself honestly and ask 'Am I *all* yours, God?' Shannon is completely vulnerable as she shares a longing for God in every area of her life and a step-by-step example of how to walk with Him in all aspects of daily living. This message is encouraging, life changing, and much needed by every one of us."
—SHAUNTI FELDHAHN, best-selling author of *For Women Only*
and *For Men Only*

Other books by Shannon Ethridge

Completely His
Completely Forgiven
Every Woman's Battle
Every Woman's Battle Workbook
Every Young Woman's Battle
Every Young Woman's Battle Workbook
Every Single Woman's Battle
Every Woman, Every Day
Every Woman's Battle Promise Book
Preparing Your Daughter for Every Woman's Battle
Every Woman's Marriage
Every Woman's Marriage Workbook
Words of Wisdom for Women at the Well
Words of Wisdom for Well Women

LOVING JESUS
A 30-DAY GUIDE
WITHOUT LIMITS

COMPLETELY
Loved

Recognizing God's Passionate Pursuit of Us

SHANNON ETHRIDGE

Best-selling author of the Every Woman's Battle series

WATERBROOK
PRESS

COMPLETELY LOVED
PUBLISHED BY WATERBROOK PRESS
12265 Oracle Boulevard, Suite 200
Colorado Springs, Colorado 80921
A division of Random House Inc.

All Scripture quotations, unless otherwise indicated, are taken from the Holy Bible, New Living Translation, copyright © 1996. Used by permission of Tyndale House Publishers Inc., Wheaton, Illinois 60189. All rights reserved. Scripture quotations marked (NIV) are taken from the Holy Bible, New International Version®. NIV®. Copyright © 1973, 1978, 1984 by International Bible Society. Used by permission of Zondervan Publishing House. All rights reserved.

Italics in Scripture quotations indicate the author's added emphasis.

Details in some anecdotes and stories have been changed to protect the identities of the persons involved.

ISBN 978-1-4000-7111-1

Library of Congress Cataloging-in-Publication Data
Ethridge, Shannon.
    Completely loved : recognizing God's passionate pursuit of us / Shannon Ethridge.—1st ed.
        p. cm.
    Includes bibliographical references and index.
    ISBN 978-1-4000-7111-1
    1. God—Love. 2. Spirituality. 3. Devotional calendars. I. Title.
    BT140.E825 2007
    242'.2—dc22

                                                            2007001538

Printed in the United States of America
2007—First Edition

10 9 8 7 6 5 4 3 2 1

SPECIAL SALES
Most WaterBrook books are available in special quantity discounts when purchased in bulk by corporations, organizations, and special-interest groups. Custom imprinting or excerpting can also be done to fit special needs. For information, please e-mail SpecialMarkets@Water BrookPress.com or call 1-800-603-7051.

CONTENTS

AN INVITATION INTO THE HEART OF GOD

I'm thrilled you're holding this little book in your hands! You're about to see God in a whole new way, recognizing aspects of His character that perhaps you've never considered before, even if you've been in relationship with Him for years.

Here's how it works: this book is the first of four devotional companions to the lead book in the series, *Completely His*. If you've not read that yet, I encourage you to do so for a look at how God is wooing and pursuing you as His spiritual bride. But if you choose to read this one first, you'll still be enriched by this devotional—and the three other devotionals in the Loving Jesus Without Limits series. That's because each one is designed to help you dive into God's Word for yourself, taking you to a deeper level of commitment to your heavenly Bridegroom, Jesus Christ. Because when it comes to God's goodness and passionate love for us, why just take someone else's word for it? Why not hear God speak directly to you from the extraordinary love letter He wrote to each of us centuries ago?

Imagine how different life could be when you experience thirty days of heart-to-heart time with God through this book, and then thirty more days in the second devotional, and so on, learning more and more about:

- how far God has gone to pursue us
  (which is the message of the devotional you are holding),
- how God can use you mightily in spite of your shortcomings
  (the message in *Completely Forgiven: Responding to God's Transforming Grace*),
- how God lavishes both His presence and His presents upon us
  (explored in *Completely Blessed: Discovering God's Extraordinary Gifts*)

- how our love for God cannot be contained, but can be shared naturally
  (examined in *Completely Irresistible: Drawing Others to God's Extravagant Love*).

I pray that as you read God's Word and go through each devotional, He will reveal Himself to you in new and magnificent ways. He wants to court you personally, building up your confidence in His character so that you'll be inspired to commit your life and love to Him without reservation and without limits—becoming completely His and enjoying a more intimate relationship with Him.

Isn't *intimate* a wonderful word? I've always loved the word *intimacy*. In fact, I love to break the word down into syllables. Look what happens when you do that:

❧ IN-TO-ME-SEE ❧

Isn't that revealing? Doesn't that make the essence of the word come alive in a new way? How we long to see the beauty in another person's heart! How we also long for someone to see the beauty in our own hearts and to value and cherish us because of what they see! Indeed, genuine intimacy is one of the deepest desires of man and woman.

But have you ever thought about why we crave intimacy?

It's because we're made in God's image, and He craves intimacy with us.

Isn't that incredible? With His supernatural eyesight, God has no problem seeing into your heart, but have you ever considered how He longs for you to see directly into His?

That's why He gave us His Word—to show us His heart for the world, His passion for His people, His longing for our worship, and His desire to be in an incredibly intimate relationship with us.

Unfortunately, we often miss these sentiments when we read the Bible. We're too focused on the forefront of the story—the human characters' situations, actions, and reactions—rather than the background of the story, where God reveals Himself.

What if, as we read the Bible, we understood that the people involved are merely God's supporting characters and that God plays the lead role in every story? We just have to look past the people and circumstances to recognize what He is doing, why, and what His actions tell us about His character. As we do, we begin to know Him more intimately, which leads us to love Him more deeply.

So that's what we'll be doing for the next thirty days: reading about several Old Testament characters and considering where God is in the story—what He is doing, why, and what that means for us. Then, through introspective questions in a section called "Holding His Hand," we'll translate this new knowledge into a deeper personal level of love and trust.

This may be a new way of reading the Bible for you. If so, I must warn you that it's addicting! And I believe that's what God desires—for us to become addicted to hearing Him speak to us every day.

I'm certain that He didn't give us this extravagant love letter to teach us about some saints and sinners who died long ago. His hope, I believe, is that through reading it, we will learn more about Him. And the more we learn about Him, the more we'll want to learn.

So are you ready to let these devotionals springboard you into a more fulfilling life of passion, purpose, and genuine intimacy with Jesus Christ?

If so, let's begin.

COMPLETELY
Loved BY...
OUR CREATOR

Daily reading: Genesis 1:1–2:25

Key passage: Then God said, "Let us make people in our image, to be like ourselves. They will be masters over all life—the fish in the sea, the birds in the sky, and all the livestock, wild animals, and small animals."

So God created people in his own image; God patterned them after himself; male and female he created them....

Then God looked over all he had made, and he saw that it was excellent in every way. (Genesis 1:26–27, 31)

Could you imagine God having His own television show on the Home & Garden Television (HGTV) network?

Talk about divine design! God doesn't just coordinate colors, textures, and patterns; He formulates them from His own vivid imagination. He designed such architectural masterpieces as the Grand Canyon, the Rocky Mountains, and Niagara Falls. He planted the most bountiful of gardens, such as the one you just read about in the second chapter of Genesis, fashioning the seeds, soil, rain, and sunshine with His own hand. Not even the most artistic of landscape or interior designers can hold a candle to what our God can do.

As I write this, I'm sitting in a window seat with a cool breeze flowing through the screen. Multiple layers of clouds glide overhead as if they are performing some graceful, slow-motion ballet against an azure blue background. I've been reflecting on the past twenty-four hours of my life and how this Creator of ours has touched me. I watched the sun rise and set yesterday and was mesmerized by many events in between.

On my morning walk I witnessed several bright red cardinals fluttering from branch to branch in the dense forest. I wondered how many pine needles and leaves could be counted on this one-hundred-acre plot of land, but imagining that number made my brain hurt. How remarkable that God can number every hair on each of our heads! What a mathematical mind our Creator has!

When I got home, my son removed a Band-Aid from his no-longer-tender foot and said, "Mom, I think it's cool how God made skin! It just heals all by itself!" Later that afternoon, my daughter and I made thumbprint cookies, and I was reminded that although billions of humans have walked the earth, no two fingerprints have ever been alike. Last night, I visited a new mom in the hospital and got to hold her little seven-pound miracle in my arms. The older I get, the more I stand in awe of certain aspects of creation—and of the incredible Creator who forms and fashions all things.

Just think: of all His magnificent creations—the brilliant sun, moon, and stars; the vast oceans; the fascinating planets; the exotic animals; and more—the one that most resembles God Himself is humankind—*you and me*. God made us *in His image;* we are as true a reflection of His character and nature as possible. Search the universe, and nothing will say "God" more than the creation known as man and woman.

Adam and Eve were the first to know this distinction, and the last to experience the fullness of being image bearers of God before sin clouded this glorious relationship. Even though we'll never walk with God on this side of heaven without sin tainting the relationship somehow, walking in relationship with Him is exactly what we were created to do. He created us for this purpose—to represent and be in relationship with our Creator God.

We find passion and joy in walking with the One who designed every part of us. He designed our minds, so He knows how to put us at ease. He created our bodies, so He knows how to strengthen us. He formed our hearts, so He knows how to thrill and delight us. He molded our spirits, so He knows our innermost desires; and only He can satisfy those desires.

Dear sister, do you agree with God that His creation is excellent in every way? What is your assessment of His handiwork when you look in the mirror? Do you see yourself as fearfully and wonderfully made by a masterful artist, as the pinnacle of His creative efforts? Do you believe God looks upon you with great satisfaction?

I hope so, because it's true. You are more precious to Him than the silver, gold, or diamonds He formed in the depths of the earth. When He sent His only Son to die on the cross, it wasn't to save the whales or the rain forests, but to save *you*. He loves you completely because you aren't just anyone; you are His special creation.

HOLDING HIS HAND

Do I believe that when God formed me, He was pleased with His handiwork?

_____

_____

_____

What does today's passage teach me about my Creator?

everything created was for His pleasure

_____

What might God want to teach me about myself?

That I am unconditionally loved by Him

_____

Creator God,

Help me to recognize Your beauty and wonder evident throughout all of creation —from the tiniest DNA molecule to the galaxies far beyond our awareness. But most of all, help me to recognize Your beauty and wonder when I look at myself.

COMPLETELY *Loved* BY...
OUR WITNESS

Daily reading: Genesis 16; 21:1–21

Key passage: Thereafter, Hagar referred to the LORD, who had spoken to her, as "the God who sees me," for she said, "I have seen the One who sees me!" (Genesis 16:13)

---

*I*magine walking in Hagar's sandals for a while. You're a slave girl who had no choice but to offer not only your services but also your body to your mistress's husband. Now you are pregnant with his child, yet his wife treats you so harshly you must run away. You are caught in quite the dilemma.

For Hagar, wandering in the desert was the lesser of the two evils. That is, until an angel appeared with a special message for her, a message that could have ticked her off. He told Hagar to return to her mistress and submit to her authority and that the child she was carrying would be "a wild one...against everyone, and everyone will be against him. Yes, he will live at odds with the rest of his brothers" (Genesis 16:12).

Would you accept such a prophecy without an argument? I doubt I could swallow this message without reciting 101 reasons why the angel should let me find more comfortable living arrangements and begging him to bless me with a more happy-go-lucky child.

Yet Scripture doesn't indicate that Hagar put up much of a fight. Her response indicates that she was at peace with her situation, regardless of how difficult it must have been. Why? Because she looked past her situation to recognize that *God actually saw her.* Her Maker knew her plight and was a witness to her life. That seemed to satisfy her; it was enough for her to simply know beyond a shadow of a doubt that God saw her and her circumstances.

Something about the human condition causes us to crave being noticed by another. If you don't believe me, consider these questions:

- Do you remember how important it was to you that your mom or dad come to the game, the play, or the performance, simply because you wanted someone to watch you?
- Were you ever a wallflower at a high-school dance, desperate for someone to invite you onto the dance floor as proof that you'd been noticed?
- Have you ever been the tiniest bit jealous of the famous Hollywood celebrity who seems to have millions of witnesses to her glamorous life?
- Have you ever gone above and beyond on a project, hoping that your professor or boss would notice your unique gifts and talents?
- Have you ever sat by the phone or walked to the mailbox, hoping that someone thought enough of you to call or write?
- Have you ever gone all out to clean your house or make a special meal, hoping that your friends or family would take special notice?

The overwhelming desire to be noticed runs deep in many of us. I believe the longing to get married someday that most of us experience is often rooted in this desire. In the movie *Shall We Dance?* Beverly Clark (played by actress Susan Sarandon) explains her theory on why people get married in the first place:

> We need a witness to our lives. There's a billion people on the planet.... I mean, what does any one life really mean? But in a

marriage, you're promising to care about *everything*. The good things, the bad things, the terrible things, the mundane things—*all* of it, *all* the time, *every* day. You're saying, "Your life will *not* go unnoticed because *I* will notice it. Your life will *not* go unwitnessed because *I* will be your witness."

While it is wonderful to have a spouse, family, or friends to witness the peaks and valleys in our lives, we often feel unnoticed in spite of the intimacy we share with others, even those who live underneath the same roof. We don't share many of our thoughts and feelings with another living soul, not because we don't want to share them, but because it's not possible for someone to witness every single aspect of another's life.

Yet there *is* one who knows my every thought, who notices every desire of my heart, and who witnesses every single moment in my life—the good, the bad, and the ugliest of moments. Even though 99 percent of these moments are rather uneventful, God truly cares about each one of them and still loves me completely.

He sees not only every part of me, but He sees you, too. Your life is not going unnoticed. God is a witness to every aspect of your every day, and He is your biggest cheerleader through every circumstance. Others may witness certain scenes, but only God sits throughout the entire production of your life, from beginning to end. Make this performance count. Remember: life is not a dress rehearsal. It's your only shot at absolutely delighting your audience of One.

HOLDING HIS HAND

Have I ever wondered if the God of the universe truly sees me? Why or why not? How does this make me feel?

_____

_____

_____

When have I ever felt desperate to know that God recognizes my plight? What was the reason?

_____

_____

_____

Do I believe that God is an active witness to every aspect of my life? What does this belief say about me?

_____

_____

_____

Dear God,

I may not understand why it feels so important to be noticed at times, but I thank You that nothing in my life goes unnoticed by You. Even though You witness my finest and worst moments, You never stop cheering me on, and for that I am eternally grateful.

Completely
Loved BY...

OUR WISE COUNSELOR

Daily reading: 1 Kings 3:3–28

Key passage: "Give me an understanding mind so that I can govern your people well and know the difference between right and wrong. For who by himself is able to govern this great nation of yours?"

The Lord was pleased with Solomon's reply and was glad that he had asked for wisdom. So God replied, "Because you have asked for wisdom in governing my people and have not asked for a long life or riches for yourself or the death of your enemies—I will give you what you asked for! I will give you a wise and understanding mind such as no one else has ever had or ever will have! And I will also give you what you did not ask for—riches and honor! No other king in all the world will be compared to you for the rest of your life!" (1 Kings 3:9–13)

---

*I*f you were to walk the city streets and poll a variety of people, how do you think most would respond to the question, "If you could have one wish, what would you ask for?"

Most would ask for things of incredibly high value or things that are just out of their reach. You'd probably hear answers such as "a million dollars," "a bigger house," "a nicer car," or "to be completely out of debt." You might hear some say that they'd like relief from a debilitating health issue or healing for a loved one. Others might give the standard Miss America response: "World peace." Still others might ask for a special someone to relate to—an emotionally available man to marry, a friend to ease their loneliness, or perhaps a baby to fill their empty arms.

If God said to you in a dream, "What do you want? Ask and I will give it to you," what would you ask for? Would you have the wisdom to ask for even more wisdom? Wisdom should be near the top of our wish list. Next to our salvation, it is one of the greatest assets we could ask for. Regardless of what role we fill as followers of Christ—wives, mothers, daughters, friends, leaders, employees, or students—wisdom is the gift that keeps on giving in every situation.

I find it interesting that after God granted Solomon wisdom, one of the king's first tests was related to parenting and children. In this dramatic moment, Solomon had to discern which of two women was the biological mother of a child. Pause for a second and realize that there was no DNA testing back then. No lie-detector tests either. This was a real game of Truth or Consequences, and Solomon needed a surefire way of asking, "Will the real mother of this child please stand up?" How did he determine who the child belonged to? He was wise enough to put the women through the "love" test. He put the baby's life on the line. He wisely understood that a mother would be willing to give another woman her child, if such a decision would spare the child's life. This was one smart move. Solomon's request for wisdom really paid off.

I remember a time when my own child's life was on the line and I desperately needed God's wisdom to discern what to do. After seven days of fluctuating fever and a croupy cough, I took Erin to the doctor for a second time. He gave her another brief exam, put her on a preventive antibiotic to keep her from getting worse, and sent us home. Erin's fever disappeared within forty-eight hours, but her cough didn't. We were pouring cough suppressants down her like crazy, just so she could get some sleep. I called the doctor and asked if I should be concerned, to which he responded, "Since she's on that preventive antibiotic, I'm not too worried. If she's not better in a few more days when she's finished her round of antibiotics, you can bring her back in."

We felt we should trust this doctor. After all, since he had graduated from medical school and had years of experience, he must be much wiser when it comes to health-care issues, right? Still, I sensed something just wasn't right, and after praying for wisdom, I decided we needed to take Erin to another doctor for a second opinion.

Dr. Vera took one look at my eleven-year-old daughter, ordered the nurse to take an oxygen-sensor test and a chest x-ray, and within five minutes returned to the exam room where he looked me in the eye and said, "Erin has a severe case of pneumonia. You have to get her to the emergency room for a breathing treatment, and you don't have time to go home first."

Cold chills ran down my spine as I gathered our things and rushed my daughter out the door for a thirty-minute car ride to the nearest hospital. Trying not to alarm her, I made a few calls to ask for prayer. Erin was admitted to the hospital through the emergency room, where we would endure five days of breathing treatments, intravenous drugs, and chest physical therapy (where the nurses tried to physically beat the mucous in her lungs loose so she could cough it up). Every doctor who reviewed her chart and examined her asked, "Do you realize how close you came to losing her?" The thought was more than any of us could bear.

Some considered my response to Erin's condition mother's intuition. I consider it divine intervention. Often we don't have all the answers. Sometimes we don't have a clue. But the God who loves us is a wise counselor who can intervene and give us the wisdom and discernment we need in every situation. Isn't it great to know that God is so infinitely wise and more than willing to share His wisdom with us, His beloved bride?

HOLDING HIS HAND

What does today's passage teach me about how God values our hunger for wisdom?

_____

_____

_____

Do I believe that God is the ultimate dispenser of the wisdom I need to handle every situation?

_____

_____

_____

Are there situations in my life in which I have failed to ask for wisdom? If so, what are they?

_____

_____

_____

> *Wise Counselor,*
>
> *All truth is Your truth, and all wisdom is Your wisdom. We ask for the serenity to accept the things we cannot change, the courage to change the things we can, and the wisdom to know the difference.*[1]

COMPLETELY
Loved BY...
OUR REDEEMER

Daily reading: Isaiah 49

Key passage: He said to me, "You are my servant, Israel, and you will bring me glory."

I replied, "But my work all seems so useless! I have spent my strength for nothing and to no purpose at all. Yet I leave it all in the LORD's hand; I will trust God for my reward." (Isaiah 49:3–4)

---

*H*ave you ever felt that even though God created you for a purpose, your work seems rather useless?

I certainly have, and many times I still do. I look back over the lofty goals I established for the day and have to transfer the bulk of them to the next calendar page. What usually prevents me from being as productive as I'd like to be? Life! Life happens, and it doesn't usually consult me to ensure it's in alignment with my personal agenda.

I've often wondered why the boring, mundane, and routine tasks of life have to take up so much of our time. For example, let's say that we live one hundred years. Now imagine where much of this time goes—eight hours of sleep each night equals 292,000 hours of our lives spent flat on our backs in bed. Three hours each day of preparing meals, eating, and cleaning up is

109,500 hours of our lives. One hour each day in the bathroom taking a shower, brushing teeth, drying hair, putting on our faces, and getting ready for the day equates to 36,500 hours. Four hours spent each week cleaning house equals 20,800 hours of our lives. Then there's the amount of time we spend in our cars getting from one place to another, on the phone or computer taking care of business, and so on.

Maybe you are thinking, *Yeah, right! I never get eight full hours of sleep a night, a full hour in the bathroom, or even four hours a week to clean my house!* Granted—certain seasons of our lives are so busy that time seems more like a luxury than a necessity, so we cram as much as we can into as little time as possible.

All these tasks need to be repeated over and over, day in and day out, year after year. Don't you sometimes wish you could clean your house one time and it would just stay that way? Or that you could fix your hair and put on your makeup, and not worry about it again until you are ready to change the style? Then we wouldn't waste precious time doing the same things over and over. Life just won't slow down long enough for us to feel as if we can really make a difference for God, right?

Perhaps it's time we look at life from a different perspective. Even people involved in full-time ministry can feel as if they are just spinning their wheels, not really making the difference they long to make in people's lives. But are we underestimating the impact we make on others by the little things we do? Aren't we reflecting God's light in a dark world when we simply smile at someone and say "Hello," which takes no time at all? Aren't we serving others when we cut the crusts off that umpteenth peanut-butter-and-jelly sandwich or poke the straw into the foil hole of the juice box so that our toddlers don't get more on their shirts than in their bellies? Don't we glorify God whenever we do even the most mundane tasks (like scrubbing the toilet seat) with care and concern for our family? Isn't obeying traffic laws a sign of our commitment to excellence and love for others? It certainly can be.

We have an almighty God who could do everything Himself, in spite of us. God doesn't need us, yet He chooses to work through us. When He created us, did He realize how much of our twenty-four-hour days would need to be invested in the mundane, just so we can get the sleep, nourishment, and self-care we need? Yes. He designed our bodies in such a way that we would need adequate amounts of rest, nutrition, and personal hygiene. On the other hand, He could have designed us to operate twenty-four hours per day without the need to sleep or eat or bathe. Then we could devote more time and attention to His service. But He didn't make us as robots without personal needs. He made us as high-maintenance humans.

Perhaps God created our daily lives to be a blessing, not just to Him and to the body of Christ, but also to us personally. Think about it. We may look at many of our daily requirements as burdens we must bear, but who of us doesn't enjoy a wonderful night's sleep or a luxurious afternoon nap on occasion? Or an incredibly flavorful meal? Or a relaxing hot shower after a long day of work? Or a clean house where we can enjoy fellowship with loved ones? Rather than viewing these things as necessary evils, can't we joyfully experience them as precious gifts from a loving God? After all, wouldn't our heavenly Bridegroom desire that His spiritual bride enjoy every aspect of life with Him, not just the work we perform for Him?

Ephesians 2:10 reminds us that "we are God's workmanship, created in Christ Jesus to do good works, which God prepared in advance for us to do" (NIV). So by all means, devote as much time and service to God as possible. But don't underestimate the power you hold to accomplish the Lord's work by being the best, most well-rounded person you can be. Don't feel guilty about the time you invest in the routine things to simply keep life working for you and those you care for. Trust that God is not only the Redeemer of your soul, but also the Redeemer of your time.

HOLDING HIS HAND

Do I look at life's routine daily requirements as my personal burdens rather than blessings from God and opportunities for genuine service?

What does today's passage teach me about my Redeemer?

_____

_____

_____

Is there something in particular God wants to say to me today through this reading? What might it be?

_____

_____

_____

> *My Precious Redeemer,*
>
> *Thank You for revealing Yourself to me in even the mundane things of life. Don't let me lose sight of the value You place on my every act of service, no matter how great or small. I trust in You, Lord, for my reward, and I ask that You allow my every waking and sleeping breath to bring You great glory.*

COMPLETELY
Loved BY...

OUR MASTER ARCHITECT

Daily reading: Isaiah 53:1–12

Key passage: But it was the LORD's good plan to crush him and fill him with grief. Yet when his life is made an offering for sin, he will have a multitude of children, many heirs. He will enjoy a long life, and the LORD's plan will prosper in his hands. When he sees all that is accomplished by his anguish, he will be satisfied. And because of what he has experienced, my righteous servant will make it possible for many to be counted righteous, for he will bear all their sins. (Isaiah 53:10–11)

What strikes you most about today's reading? Was it that Jesus was treated so harshly? That He silently submitted to the cruelty of His persecutors? That we are the beneficiaries of His suffering, even though we are the sinful ones and Jesus was completely without sin?

While all of these things are certainly striking (there's no wrong answer to the above question!), what strikes me most is that this passage comes from the book of Isaiah. Why is this so startling? Because Isaiah lived from 740 to 681 BC, hundreds of years before Jesus was born. All of what you just read from the Scriptures today is prophecy—a divine foretelling of what the future held in regard to God's salvation story.

How did Isaiah know these things would come to pass as accurately as he envisioned? Because Isaiah received these words directly from God, the Master Architect who carefully planned every detail of our redemption from day one, even before Creation. Nothing about Jesus' life or the atonement for humanity happened accidentally. As God built the foundations of the earth, He had the blueprints in mind as to how He would accomplish His greatest feat, restoring sinful humanity to Himself and providing a way for the church, His spiritual bride, to live in an intimate relationship with Him for all eternity.

My family and I discovered the importance of having a plan when we embarked on a massive building and remodeling project on our log cabin. Initially, we hired a pricey architect who promised to draw a seamless plan for adding on to our home. We eventually fired him because the best drawings he had produced didn't look much better than a stick-house scribbled in crayon on a napkin. Then God led us to another architect, who knew exactly what he was doing. For a fraction of what we had already paid the previous architect, this one created a computerized blueprint that allowed us to see a three-dimensional view of the house, including every room, every window, and every nook and cranny. After months of planning, we felt confident that the blueprint reflected our desires, so we handed it off to a professional builder who executed every aspect of that plan with great attention to detail. What resulted is a masterpiece, an amazing house that exceeds our wildest dreams.

God is a lot like our second architect, only better. He knows exactly what He's doing, and throughout the Bible He provides us with vivid portrayals of Himself and His perfect plan so that we can understand His character and His intentions. He handed His plan over to Jesus, who executed every aspect just as God desired (and just as the prophets foretold long ago). The result is a masterpiece far beyond our wildest dreams—we get to dwell in the house of the Lord forever.

It's simply human nature to feel more secure following someone with a clear plan than someone with no clue. Girlfriend, God is the ultimate Man with the Plan, a plan that has unfolded throughout history and will continue to unfold throughout eternity. So if you desire a future beyond your wildest dreams, follow the Master Architect. He will pour a solid foundation of character into your life. He will construct many opportunities for you to feel intimately connected with Him. He will shelter you with His loving care. He will stretch you and help you become more than you ever thought you could be. Best of all, He has already built you a beautiful heavenly mansion, a place where you get to bask in His presence forever.

HOLDING HIS HAND

Am I truly following God's plan for my salvation, or am I depending on someone or something else for my sense of eternal security? How do I know the difference?

What does today's passage teach me about the Master Architect of my salvation?

What might I learn about myself through today's reading?

Dear God,

You are the Man with the Plan! There is no other way to You, Father, except through Your Son, Jesus Christ! Thank You for Your divine plan for my salvation, and thank You that You've already constructed an incredibly secure future for me alongside You in heaven.

COMPLETELY
Loved BY...

OUR CONSTANT
COMPANION

Daily reading: Genesis 5

Key passage: When Enoch was 65, his son Methuselah was born. After the birth of Methuselah, Enoch lived another 300 years in close fellowship with God, and he had other sons and daughters. Enoch lived 365 years in all. He enjoyed a close relationship with God throughout his life. Then suddenly, he disappeared because God took him. (Genesis 5:21–24)

Growing up, I heard lots of Bible stories about biblical heroes—Abraham, Isaac, Jacob, David, Esther, and so on, but I never heard one story about Enoch. I probably read right past his only mention in the Bible several times before it hit me that he was, in fact, a hero as well.

What made Enoch so great? He didn't lead an army into battle. He didn't erect a huge monument to God (at least not that we know of from Scripture). He didn't boldly stand before kings, nor was he persecuted for his faith (again, not we know of). So what was so great about Enoch? He knew how to live. He knew what was so wonderful about fellowship with God. He wasn't a rebel, nor did he struggle with his faith. "He enjoyed a close relationship with God *throughout his life*" (Genesis 5:24).

Oh, how I wish the same could be said about me—that I followed Enoch's example and enjoyed a close relationship with God every single day of my life. However, I spent many days walking further and further away from God (sometimes running from Him) rather than walking closely beside Him each day. What I wouldn't give to have the opportunity to relive those days and walk hand in hand with my Savior when I needed His strength the most.

Now this next sentence about Enoch is a real attention grabber! "Then suddenly, he *disappeared* because God *took* him" (Genesis 5:24). Hello! Enoch did what? He just disappeared? You mean he didn't die a natural death? He just checked out of Hotel Earth and into eternity without any pain or suffering? Why would God just *take* Enoch?

Hebrews 11:5 tells us, "It was by faith that Enoch was taken up to heaven without dying—'suddenly he disappeared because God took him.' But before he was taken up, he was approved as pleasing to God." Can you imagine living a life of faith that was so pleasing to God that He would invite you to spend eternity with Him without even dying?

I once heard a child explain it best. Retelling the story in his own words, he said, "Enoch and God were such good buddies and walked together every day, until finally God said, 'You know, Enoch, we're closer to my house than we are to yours, so what do you say we just go on to my house?'" My interpretation of this account is similar—that God simply delighted in Enoch so much that He wanted them to be as close as possible, so He invited Enoch on a one-way, all-expenses-paid trip to the mansion next-door to His.

As I contemplate what "walking with God" on a regular basis means, I am reminded of the three-year period in which I took frequent walks with a dear friend before she moved across the country. Although we benefited from the exercise, the real prize was the intimate friendship we cultivated during those times together. However, there were weeks when it was too cold or rainy or one of our kids was sick and we couldn't get outside. During those weeks, we missed each other sorely, and now the void is even greater with the geographical distance that separates us. However, we never have to miss our intimate time with God because of distance or His lack of availability. Regardless of the weather or circumstances, He is a constant companion who is forever merely a thought away.

Another thing that I find interesting about Enoch is who his son was—Methuselah. Have you ever heard the saying, "He's as old as Methuselah"? In fact, Methuselah, the oldest person mentioned in the Bible, lived to be 969 years old. That's almost three times as old as his father, who walked the earth only 365 years. It's almost thirty times as old as Jesus, who was crucified at age thirty-three. Methuselah was a man blessed with good health and a long, productive life. Could it be that the Lord's favor of Enoch spilled over into his children's lives? Perhaps. It stands to reason that the closer we walk with God, the more vivid an example our children have to follow in developing an intimate relationship with God themselves.

What about you? Is God your constant companion? Do others, especially your children or those closest to you, recognize that you are close to God? Can the effects of His sweet company be seen in your countenance? While we may not be bold enough to expect that, like Enoch, we'll never taste death, we can make the wise choice that Enoch made. We can choose to walk and talk intimately with God every single day of whatever is left of our lives.

HOLDING HIS HAND

How often do I feel as if I truly walk and/or talk with God?

_____

_____

_____

How do I know when I've experienced His sweet presence? Can others tell a difference when I've spent time with Him?

_____

_____

_____

What does today's passage teach me about God's desire to be my close companion?

_____

_____

_____

In what ways am I like Enoch, and in what ways do I still aspire to be like him?

_____

_____

_____

Dearest Lord,

Thank You that You earnestly desire to be my close companion. I appreciate the fact that You are never too tired or too busy to walk and talk with me. Draw me to Your side as often as You like, and allow me to bask in Your presence as we fellowship together.

COMPLETELY
Loved BY...

OUR REFUGE

Daily reading: Genesis 6:5–8:22

Key passage: Now the LORD observed the extent of the people's wickedness, and he saw that all their thoughts were consistently and totally evil. So the LORD was sorry he had ever made them. It broke his heart.... But Noah found favor with the LORD....

Noah was a righteous man, the only blameless man living on earth at the time. He consistently followed God's will and enjoyed a close relationship with him. (Genesis 6:5–6, 8–9)

Today we read about the great-grandson of Enoch, Noah, who was also noted for walking closely with the Lord. His name means "rest" or "comfort," as he was obviously a person who took great comfort in his intimate relationship with God, even to the point of obedience to the seemingly absurd.

Perhaps you heard this story over and over as a child and never recognized the preposterousness of what God asked Noah to do. For 120 years of his life, Noah diligently labored to build a boat of unimaginable proportions. Approximating the cubit to be a minimum of 17.5 inches, the ark had a deck measuring 95,700 square feet (almost two acres), a volume of 1,396,000 cubic feet, and a height of 45 feet, and it weighed in at 13,960 tons!

I realized the magnitude of such a ship when I recently visited the campus of Biola University in La Mirada, California, as one of the dormitories is somewhat equivalent in size to the dimensions of the ark. I commented, "No wonder it took Noah 120 years to build it!" to which our tour guide responded, "And he didn't have Black & Decker—only Arm & Hammer!" Building the ark was no small feat for Noah's hands to accomplish. Surely God was with him day by day.

In addition to building such an enormous vessel, Noah urged the people to repent of their wicked ways. How many converts did he have at the end of a twelve-decade preaching ministry? None. Zero. Zip. Zilch. Nada. Never a single notch in his evangelism belt. Yet he continued to build without wavering, confident that what God said He would do, He would in fact do.

What's astounding about Noah's steadfast belief that a flood would eventually come is that up until this time, there is no biblical record of rainfall. Can you imagine the scoffing Noah endured as he and his family spent all those years and used all those resources to build a boat when he didn't even live near the water? Surely the thought was unimaginable—to all but Noah and his family, of course.

While Noah's role in this story seems to be the lead, let's consider the true star of this show. What do we see God doing throughout this scenario? First, we see that He was grieving heavily over the wickedness that prevailed in the hearts of humanity. Judgment was inevitable, yet notice God's patience. He waited 120 years for people's hearts to change. He longed for them to walk in intimate fellowship with Him, as Noah did, but no one showed an interest.

We also see that God recognized the purity of Noah's heart and went to great lengths to provide for his safety. He revealed His future plans to Noah and gave him detailed instructions as to how he should build the ark in order to withstand the imminent flood. In Genesis 6:20, the animals are divinely drawn to the ark in time for all to climb aboard, and in Genesis 7:16 the Lord

Himself shuts the door once Noah's family and the animals are all safely inside. What we see throughout this story is that God cannot tolerate wickedness and rebellion, and He goes to great lengths to supernaturally protect the righteous. While His desire is that not even one should perish, He takes care of those who trust in Him.

Let's move this story closer to home. If while walking in the wilderness you were caught in a torrential downpour, would you not look for a place of refuge? If you found an empty cave or a canopy of thick trees, wouldn't you take shelter from the storm? Of course you would.

Spiritually speaking, we all are walking in a wilderness. This world is full of sin, rebellion, and opportunities for us to feed our flesh. We need to find shelter in order to remain safe from harm. We need an ark in which to take refuge from the flood. And just as God provided one for Noah, He provides a place of refuge for us today. Where is this refuge? In Christ.

John 3:16–18 makes it crystal clear that Christ's purpose in coming to earth was to save the world. Why? Because God loved the world. He still loves the world. He loves every nation, every tribe, every individual. He loves you, and just as He drew Noah from the storm into the ark, He's inviting you into the only place of refuge that will suffice against the storms of life.

If you haven't already done so, follow Noah's example. Come into Christ's loving shelter. There you will find not only safety from tribulations and temptations, but also rest and comfort in your heavenly Bridegroom's arms.

HOLDING HIS HAND

Do I believe that God is eager to judge the sins of the world (mine included), or do I believe that God patiently longs for the hearts of mankind to turn toward Him? Why do I believe the way I do?

Is there anything in my life that is hindering my ability to hear the voice of the Lord as He tries to shelter me from sin?

_____

_____

_____

Is my refuge found in Christ alone, or do I turn to other things for shelter from the storms of life?

_____

_____

_____

Lord Jesus,

We stand in awe of how patient You are with sinful man-kind. Thank You for being our refuge from the storms of life. Because of the sacrifice You made, we have full confidence that we shall not perish but have everlasting life with You.

COMPLETELY
Loved BY...

OUR ROCK-SOLID
CONFIDENCE

Daily reading: 1 Kings 17:1–7; 18

Key passage: At the customary time for offering the evening sacrifice, Elijah the prophet walked up to the altar and prayed, "O LORD, God of Abraham, Isaac, and Jacob, prove today that you are God in Israel and that I am your servant. Prove that I have done all this at your command. O LORD, answer me! Answer me so these people will know that you, O LORD, are God and that you have brought them back to yourself."

Immediately the fire of the LORD flashed down from heaven and burned up the young bull, the wood, the stones, and the dust. It even licked up all the water in the ditch! And when the people saw it, they fell on their faces and cried out, "The LORD is God! The LORD is God!" (1 Kings 18:36–39)

In yesterday's reading, God unleashed an enormous rainstorm that lasted forty days and nights. In today's reading, He withholds rain, not just for forty days and nights, but for three long years. Why? So that Elijah could prove a point—that the Lord was indeed the God of heaven and earth, and that Baal was nothing but a false god that King Ahab, hundreds of prophets, and many others were worshiping in vain. Rightfully so, our heavenly Bridegroom is jealous for the faithful affections of His spiritual bride.

What strikes me about Elijah is the boldness with which he declared his prophecies. Notice he didn't say, "Have you ever considered that the Lord might withhold rain?" or "It's possible that there could be no more rain until I say so." Instead, he confidently declared, "As surely as the LORD, the God of Israel, lives—the God whom I worship and serve—there will be no dew or rain during the next few years unless I give the word!" (1 Kings 17:1).

Elijah wasn't just putting his own reputation on the line, he was putting God's reputation on the line as well. Did he have any doubts that God would come through for him? Not a chance. How could Elijah speak so confidently? Because he knew the Lord that intimately. He had allowed himself to be courted by the Creator, and because of what He knew about God, he had an unshakable confidence in Him.

When *we* allow ourselves to be courted by the Creator, we develop a similar confidence. We won't worry about whether God will come through for us; we will know He is in our corner.

In addition, Elijah wasn't putting just reputations on the line. He was putting his life on the line as well. He was already very unpopular with the crowd, especially King Ahab. After all, they credited him with their three-year drought. Elijah added insult to injury when he mocked them with comments like, "You'll have to shout louder... for surely [Baal] is a god! Perhaps he is deep in thought, or he is relieving himself. Or maybe he is away on a trip, or he is asleep and needs to be wakened!" (1 Kings 18:27). After such sarcasm, surely Elijah would have been killed on the spot had things not gone his way.

But things did go Elijah's way, and the fire of the Lord flashed down from heaven and consumed the bull, the wood, the stones, the water, and even the dust! After this dramatic demonstration of God's power and sovereignty, Elijah had all 450 prophets of Baal slaughtered.

Not only did God respond to Elijah's request to send down fire from heaven, but He also sent rain once Elijah gave the word. Can you imagine having so much clout with God that He responds to your requests for supernatural demonstrations of His power? Obviously God and Elijah were pretty tight, and God blessed Elijah with a rock-solid confidence that astounds even the boldest of preachers, evangelists, and missionaries today. (Elijah's confidence did wane temporarily shortly after this experience, but we'll discuss that in the second devotional in the series.)

Why did God respond to Elijah's extraordinary request? I believe it was because Elijah had the most honorable of motives behind his mission. Notice Elijah said, "Answer me *so these people will know that you, O LORD, are God and that you have brought them back to yourself*" (1 Kings 18:37). This powerful demonstration wasn't about Elijah glorifying himself; it was about Elijah glorifying God. Did God want to reveal Himself to the people as the one and only living God? Absolutely. And because Elijah's heart and God's heart were in accord, God could have as much confidence in Elijah as Elijah had in God.

Are you are in need of rock-solid confidence? The answer isn't in trying to produce more faith. The answer is in getting to know God more intimately, for He is truly the source of all the confidence you could ever need.

HOLDING HIS HAND

When I set out to do something in the Lord's name, do I have pure motives behind my mission? Is my goal always to glorify my God?

_____

_____

_____

Can I have the same boldness and confidence that Elijah had whenever I'm doing that which God has asked me to do? Why or why not?

_____

_____

_____

What does my response to the previous question say about God? What does it say about my personal belief in Him?

_____

_____

_____

Dearest Lord,

Thank You for trusting me to wear Your name tag. Help me represent You well, listening carefully to Your voice and obeying all that You ask of me. Give me the confidence and boldness that You gave to Elijah, and reveal Yourself to others through me.

COMPLETELY

Loved BY...

OUR SOURCE OF POWER

Daily reading: 1 Kings 17:8–24; 2 Kings 2:1–15; 4:1–37

Key passage: Then Elijah folded his cloak together and struck the water with it. The river divided, and the two of them went across on dry ground!

When they came to the other side, Elijah said to Elisha, "What can I do for you before I am taken away?"

And Elisha replied, "Please let me become your rightful successor." (2 Kings 2:8–9)

---

*Y*ou may get a feeling of déjà vu when reading today's passages, as we see that Elisha definitely received his wish to become Elijah's rightful successor. Elisha performed miracles so similar to Elijah's that his credibility is unquestionable. For instance:

- Elijah parted the water with a strike of his cloak (2 Kings 2:8), then Elisha parted the same river with the same cloak after Elijah was whisked up to heaven in a chariot of fire (2 Kings 2:14).
- Elijah multiplied oil and flour for a widow in order to save her and her son from starvation (1 Kings 17:10–16). Later we see Elisha multiplying oil for a widow in order to save her sons from slavery to her creditors (2 Kings 4:1–7).

- Elijah stretched himself out over a dead boy three times, bringing him back to life for his mother (1 Kings 17:21–22). Elisha also stretched himself across a boy's corpse twice, restoring life to his dead body and joy to his mother's heart (2 Kings 4:32–35).

How is it that Elisha had powers so similar to Elijah's? Because they both looked to God as the source of their power, and the miracles they performed were in line with God's purposes. They weren't in pursuit of power for power's sake. They were in pursuit of God Himself, not of the power that He could give them.

Let's step into the story on the day Elijah is taken up to heaven. Elisha seems determined to remain by Elijah's side. Three times Elijah suggests that they part company, yet all three times Elisha will hear nothing of it. Elijah sees Elisha's determination to continue walking alongside him and finally asks the loaded question, "What can I do for you before I am taken away?"

Elisha knows what his master is asking and just what he wants. Elisha desires to continue Elijah's ministry as God's chosen prophet to the Israelites and to do it exceedingly well. He requests not only Elijah's mantle of ministry but also a double portion of his spirit. Upon Elijah's disappearance, Elisha not only picks up Elijah's cloak and mantle but also picks up exactly where Elijah left off as God's messenger.

Like Elijah, Elisha was intimately connected to his Creator and looked to Him for wisdom and for power. Had Elisha simply been looking for power apart from God, or had he expected to receive power from Elijah himself, he would have come up empty-handed. God sees the motivation behind our actions and desires, and when our intention is aligned with His, and we truly desire to bring glory to God for God's sake (rather than for our own sake), God will not withhold His power from us.

Wisely, Elisha looked to God for strength during times of solitude with the Lord, and his faith grew as he experienced God making provision for him and performing miracles through him. Can we say the same? Are we drawing strength through times of solitude with God? Are we trusting Him to provide for us and perform miracles through us? Are we allowing ourselves to be courted by our Creator so that we can know the fullness of His power and love?

It's one thing to read about what God can do. It's another thing entirely to ask God to do those same things *through us*. As we experience God's provision and power, surely we will know beyond doubt that He is our ultimate source of power.

HOLDING HIS HAND

Who are the people I spend the most time watching, listening to, and gleaning from? What exactly do I learn from them?

_____

_____

_____

_____

_____

Have I made the mistake of looking to other people as the source of power rather than looking to God Himself? Why or why not?

_____

_____

_____

_____

_____

Do I spend enough time with God to truly reflect His character and do the things that He would have me do in order to represent Him well? Why or why not?

_____

_____

_____

Dear God,

Thank You for Your Word that gives me a much clearer picture of who You are and for Your power that You wish to manifest through me when I seek to do Your will. Teach me how to be all that You created me to be. Draw me into Your presence where I can bask in Your love and learn more of Your ways.

COMPLETELY *Loved* BY...

OUR TRUSTWORTHY FATHER

Daily reading: Genesis 22:1–18

Key passage: Then the angel of the LORD called again to Abraham from heaven, "This is what the LORD says: Because you have obeyed me and have not withheld even your beloved son, I swear by my own self that I will bless you richly. I will multiply your descendants into countless millions, like the stars of the sky and the sand on the seashore. They will conquer their enemies, and through your descendants, all the nations of the earth will be blessed—all because you have obeyed me." (Genesis 22:15–18)

---

*N*ever will we see on any big screen or in any best-selling novel a more tension-filled, suspenseful moment than we see right here in the pages of Genesis. Each time I read about this test of Abraham's trust and loyalties, I feel as if I'm sitting on the edge of my seat, even though I know the story by heart. I long to reach out and grab Abraham's arm at that pivotal moment and say, "Wait! Stop! Don't do it! Don't sacrifice your son!"

This is one test no parent would ever want to take. But I pray that regardless of the tests we face in life, we're able to pass them with flying colors the way Abraham passed this one. He had already sent his first son (Ishmael) away at Sarah's request. Now the Lord wants him to sacrifice his and Sarah's only biological child? Isn't Isaac the "child of promise," the son through whom God intended to multiply and bless all of Abraham's future generations?

Indeed he was, and somehow Abraham knew that the promise would not be destroyed. In Genesis 22, he seems eager to carry out the Lord's instructions to take the boy, go to Moriah, and sacrifice him there. We see Abraham getting up early, saddling up the necessary instruments for such a sacrifice, and traveling for three days to get to the mountain, which was fifty to sixty miles away. Abraham meticulously obeys the Lord's every instruction. He also demonstrates great faith that Isaac will either be delivered or resurrected, as he says to his servants, "We will worship there, and then *we* will come right back" (Genesis 22:5).

While we may envision that this scenario involves a young child who is too naive to fathom what is really happening, such is not the case. Isaac is old enough to make a three-day journey on a donkey, wise enough to ask about the lamb for the sacrifice (he's obviously gone through this routine many times), and strong enough to carry the wood up the mountain. Surely he was old enough to resist being bound and placed on a sacrificial altar, yet he willingly submitted to his father's will. Why? Because he trusted his father completely, just as Abraham trusted his heavenly Father completely, as he demonstrated by his strict obedience.

Many theologians agree that the purpose of this story is twofold. First, we are challenged to ponder the question, "Do I trust God enough to sacrifice my nearest and dearest treasure as Abraham did?" Perhaps your Isaac is a ministry, a career, your bank account, or something else. If God asked you to lay down your Isaac, could you? Do you trust that He only asks of us that which will ultimately benefit us?

But the greater purpose of the story is to set the stage for the ultimate sacrifice that God made in sending His own Son to die. As Abraham was pleased with Isaac, but did not withhold him, so God was pleased with Jesus (see

Matthew 3:17) and did not withhold Him either. Isaac carried the wood for his sacrifice, just as Jesus carried his cross to Calvary. As Isaac yielded himself to his father's will, even to the point of laying down his own life, Jesus yielded Himself to His Father's will to the point of death on a cross. Just as God provided a sacrificial ram as a substitute for Isaac, God gave Jesus as the sacrificial lamb to substitute for our sins.

In the story of Abraham and Isaac, we have an incredibly graphic foreshadowing of the passionate, selfless love that our heavenly Father has for us in sacrificing His only Son, Jesus Christ, for our sake. Surely there is no irony in the fact that these two scenarios have very similar endings as well. Abraham was promised that rich blessings were in store for him, his descendants, and all the nations of the earth because of his obedience to his heavenly Father's will. And because of the obedience of Christ to His Father's will, astoundingly rich blessings are in store for us as well.

HOLDING HIS HAND

Can I trust that God only asks of me that which ultimately benefits me? Why or why not?

_____

_____

_____

How has God demonstrated His trustworthiness to me in the past?

_____

_____

_____

What hard thing is God asking me to trust Him about today? Do I feel confident that I can lay down my fears and trust His direction?

_____

_____

_____

Heavenly Father,

I praise You for the incomprehensible sacrifice You made especially for me—the sacrifice of Your own beloved Son on a cross at Calvary. Lord, let nothing ever prevent me from eagerly obeying Your every request. Give me a heart to put You first in my life above everything and everyone else, for I know that You alone are completely trustworthy.

COMPLETELY
Loved BY...

OUR GUARANTOR
OF SUCCESS

Daily reading: Genesis 24:1–67

Key passage: As he was still praying, a young woman named Rebekah arrived with a water jug on her shoulder. Her father was Bethuel, who was the son of Abraham's brother Nahor and his wife, Milcah. Now Rebekah was very beautiful, and she was a virgin; no man had ever slept with her. She went down to the spring, filled her jug, and came up again. Running over to her, the servant asked, "Please give me a drink."

"Certainly, sir," she said, and she quickly lowered the jug for him to drink. When he had finished, she said, "I'll draw water for your camels, too, until they have had enough!" (Genesis 24:15–19)

After the death of his wife, Sarah, Abraham realized it was time to tend to one last order of business before he died too. He wanted to find a godly wife for his son, so that God's promise could be extended to his future generations.

This was a huge responsibility to pass on to a servant. After all, Isaac was the first heir of God's promise, the firstborn of the nation that would be called

"God's chosen people." Not just any wife would do. Could a young woman be found within Abraham's family who would be willing to leave her home, family, and friends? One who would go on a five-hundred-mile journey on a camel's back with a man she had just met? One willing to marry a man she did not know at all? This mission probably seemed equivalent to finding a needle in a haystack. The servant even asked, "But suppose I can't find a young woman willing to come back with me?" (Genesis 24:39).

Abraham's faith must have been contagious as he confidently responded, "You will,... for the LORD, in whose presence I have walked, will send his angel with you and will make your mission successful. Yes, you must get a wife for my son from among my relatives, from my father's family" (verse 40). The message was clear: God would go before Abraham's servant in order to choose Isaac's bride.

How did Abraham know that his servant would have success? Because of Abraham's intimate relationship with the Lord. He had heard the voice of God in the matter and was merely acting on what the Lord had told him to do. Abraham was following God's leading in faith, and God would not allow him to fail. God guarantees our success when we follow His leading as well.

Two qualities strike me about Abraham's servant: his loyalty to his master and his incredible faith in God to show him the exact woman He had chosen. These qualities are evident as he prays,

> O LORD, God of my master... Give me success and show kindness to my master, Abraham. Help me to accomplish the purpose of my journey. See, here I am, standing beside this spring, and the young women of the village are coming out to draw water. This is my request. I will ask one of them for a drink. If she says, "Yes, certainly, and I will water your camels, too!"—let her be the one you have appointed as Isaac's wife. By this I will know that you have shown kindness to my master. (Genesis 24:12–14)

Obviously the servant's prayer got God's attention as well, for He responded immediately with the signs the servant asked for, all before he had even said, "Amen!"

Rebekah's response to meeting this stranger is also striking. Her offer to water his ten camels until they had their fill would require a significant investment of time and labor. Remember, camels don't just take a quick sip. A camel drinks and drinks to store up water for later nourishment. Surely this chore would require several trips to the well, carrying heavy buckets of water, yet Rebekah offered to do it with a happy heart.

Several people in the story demonstrated their belief that God Himself orchestrated the success of this mission—the narrator (verses 15–16), the servant (verses 26–27), Laban and Bethuel (verse 50), and Rebekah (verse 58). I believe her willingness to disregard the wishes of her family and leave with the servant immediately indicates her faith that this situation was indeed God's handiwork.

It seems no accident that the blessings given to Rebekah and Isaac by their families were practically identical to the blessing God gave Isaac's father. Earlier, in Genesis 22:17, an angel of the Lord told Abraham, "I will multiply your descendants into countless millions, like the stars of the sky and the sand on the seashore. They will conquer their enemies." Then, in today's passage we read that Rebekah's family said to her upon her departure, "Our sister, may you become the mother of many millions! May your descendants overcome all their enemies" (Genesis 24:60). Clearly, the marital union of Isaac and Rebekah was literally a match made in heaven.

As stirring as this passage is, this is not just a beautiful love story. It's also an allegory of an even greater love story. Abraham represents God the Father seeking a wife for His Son. Isaac represents Jesus Christ as the Bridegroom waiting for His bride to be brought to Him by His father. Abraham's servant is a representation of the Holy Spirit, who draws us away from our past life into a new life of purity and promise. And Rebekah symbolizes the believer as she submits herself and her future into the hands of the Holy Spirit, her anticipated Bridegroom, and her heavenly Father.

We, too, are being courted by the Creator. God longs for us to be part of the collective bride of Christ that He will present to His Son at the wedding supper of the Lamb. He has sent His Holy Spirit to woo us and pursue us into a love relationship with our Bridegroom. Will you, like Rebekah, allow yourself to be drawn toward your divine destiny? Will you follow God's lead-ing in faith, trusting Him as the guarantor of your success in life?

HOLDING HIS HAND

How could Abraham and his servant have so much faith that God would turn this "mission impossible" into a complete success?

_____

_____

_____

What seemingly impossible missions am I facing today? Do I believe that God can give me success as I trust and follow Him? Why or why not?

_____

_____

_____

What characteristics do I have in common with Rebekah? Have I completely left my old life behind in anticipation of an even greater life with my heav-enly Bridegroom?

_____

_____

_____

Heavenly Father,

Thank You that we do not have to fear failure! I praise You for granting us success in every mission You call us to. I am in awe that You would choose me to be the beloved bride of Your Son, and that You would send Your Holy Spirit to draw me into a love relationship with Him. Thank You for inviting me to the wedding supper of the Lamb, not just as a guest, but as the bride!

COMPLETELY

Loved BY...

OUR SOURCE OF BLESSINGS

Daily reading: Genesis 26:1–33

Key passage: From there Isaac moved to Beersheba, where the LORD appeared to him on the night of his arrival. "I am the God of your father, Abraham," he said. "Do not be afraid, for I am with you and will bless you. I will give you many descendants, and they will become a great nation. I will do this because of my promise to Abraham, my servant." Then Isaac built an altar there and worshiped the LORD. He set up his camp at that place, and his servants dug a well. (Genesis 26:23–25)

---

*I*f God told you something once, you'd have a tendency to believe it, right? What if He told you twice? Would your faith in what He was saying and your ability to hear Him increase? Most likely.

In this chapter of Genesis, we find God promising to bless Isaac not just once but twice. Let's rewind the tape for an instant replay:

- The LORD appeared to [Isaac in Gerar] and said, "Do not go to Egypt. Do as I say, and stay here in this land. If you do, I will be with you and bless you. I will give all this land to you and your descendants, just as I solemnly promised Abraham, your father. I will cause your descendants to become as

numerous as the stars, and I will give them all these lands.
And through your descendants all the nations of the earth
will be blessed. I will do this because Abraham listened to
me and obeyed all my requirements, commands, regulations,
and laws." (Genesis 26:2–5)

- From there Isaac moved to Beersheba, where the LORD
appeared to him on the night of his arrival. "I am the God
of your father, Abraham," he said. "Do not be afraid, for I
am with you and will bless you. I will give you many descendants, and they will become a great nation. I will do this
because of my promise to Abraham, my servant." (Genesis
26:23–24)

In this chapter, we can also see that Isaac and his father have a lot in common. Just as God promised Abraham certain blessings, in Genesis 26 He
promises Isaac the same blessings: his descendents will be numerous, the
Promised Land will be his, and all nations will be blessed through him.

It appears that God loved Isaac not only because of who he was, but also
because of who his parents were. However, children need their own special
revelation of who God is, and we sense that God didn't want Isaac resting on
his father's laurels, because He gave His promises directly to Isaac (in addition
to the promise previously given to Abraham). God wanted Isaac to have a
personal experience with Him. He desires the same for us. Regardless of who
our parents are or what kind of relationship they have with the Lord, we must
seek a relationship with Him that is uniquely personal to us. We must be
courted personally by our Creator, not by proxy through relatives. God wants
to interact with us directly and personally, not through someone else.

Not only do we see Isaac receiving the same promises and blessings his
father received, but we also see in this chapter that he repeated his father's
offense. Fearing that the men of Gerar would kill him in order to possess his
beautiful wife, Isaac lied and said that Rebekah was his sister. (In Genesis
20:2, Abraham told the same lie about his wife, Sarah, for the same reason.)

Yet God still honored His promise to bless Isaac. Even after Isaac lied about Rebekah, the chapter reports, "That year Isaac's crops were tremendous! He harvested a hundred times more grain than he planted, for the LORD blessed him. He became a rich man, and his wealth only continued to grow. He acquired large flocks of sheep and goats, great herds of cattle, and many servants" (Genesis 26:12–14). What a vivid reminder that God's goodness isn't dependent upon our goodness! He often chooses to bless people simply for following Him, even when we occasionally choose the wrong course of action. How reassuring that we don't lose His favor whenever we stumble and fall in the wrong direction.

Finally, another insight we can glean from this passage is how to respond to interpersonal conflict. Just as Abraham responded humbly to the conflict that arose between him and Lot as a result of their combined prosperity, so Isaac responded humbly to the conflict that arose as a result of the Philistines' envy of his prosperity. When he moved to the Valley of Gerar, he reopened his father's wells, which the Philistines had filled with dirt. However, when his servants dug a fresh well, the shepherds of Gerar insisted that the water from this well belonged to them. Instead of retaliating, Isaac relinquished the well and opened another well, without showing signs of discouragement. Once again the shepherds claimed the well, and once again Isaac moved on and didn't retaliate.

When he dug a third well, the shepherds finally left him alone. However, they eventually sought him out to make a covenant of peace with him, to which Isaac responded by forgiving them and hosting a great feast in honor of their new peace treaty. Isaac's soft answers obviously turned away their wrath (a promise made in Proverbs 15:1). This story also supports the proverb, "When the ways of people please the LORD, he makes even their enemies live at peace with them" (Proverbs 16:7).

Are you eager to live at peace with your enemies? To experience God's favor in spite of your shortcomings? To have an intimate personal relationship directly with God? If so, trust in the same source of blessings that Abraham and Isaac trusted in—the Lord God Almighty, maker of heaven and earth.

HOLDING HIS HAND

Do I put too much stock in my family's relationship with God rather than pursuing a unique, personal relationship with Him myself?

Do I truly believe that God desires to bless me, in spite of my sin and short-comings?

Am I living at peace with everyone around me, or do I need the Lord to grant me discernment for how to respond to someone who is causing me grief?

Dear God,

Thank You for the numerous lessons that we can learn from Isaac's life and how You chose to bless him in spite of his sin. Give us a personal revelation of Your mercy, Your grace, and Your generosity toward Your beloved. Help us to radiate Your love to those around us as we strive to live in peace even with our enemies.

COMPLETELY
Loved BY...

OUR ADVOCATE

Daily reading: Numbers 27:1–11; 36

Key passage: So Moses brought their case before the LORD. And the LORD replied to Moses, "The daughters of Zelophehad are right. You must give them an inheritance of land along with their father's relatives. Assign them the property that would have been given to their father." (Numbers 27:5–7)

Before Lady Godiva rode naked through the streets of Coventry to bring tax relief to the people of England...before Joan of Arc freed her country from English domination and became a national heroine of France and saint of the Catholic Church...before Susan B. Anthony led the effort to secure a woman's right to vote in the United States...there were Zelophehad's five daughters.

These women were trailblazers for sure. No woman had ever before brought a land dispute into the courts. Such unprecedented action required an incredible amount of courage, faith, and determination. Where did these women get these qualities? Most likely from the Lord Himself, for God used these women to bless other women for many generations to come, including yours and mine. Zelophehad's daughters felt strongly that they should inherit land that would have been given to their deceased father, and they must have believed that the Lord would be their advocate and secure for them their rightful inheritance.

By the time these women presented their case to Moses, they had most likely already gone through the proper chain of command with no success. In keeping with his father-in-law's advice, Moses had delegated leaders to represent smaller groups rather than hearing every single case himself (Exodus 18:13–26). So, it's likely these women had already approached other delegated leaders, but none of them would make a decision in the case—perhaps because they didn't feel they had the authority to make such an unconventional ruling. Finally, the daughters' plea reached the highest authority in Israel, and Moses wisely looked to God for guidance in the complicated matter.

The Lord not only granted Zelophehad's daughters their request, He went above and beyond what they were asking. Their petition was for land (Numbers 27:4), but they were also granted a hereditary possession of that land. Not only could they live on the property, they could also bequeath it to their heirs as well. It was as if their father had sons.[1] However, in light of this new law, a potential conflict loomed large over the nation of Israel. The tribal land divisions were supposed to remain unmixed, yet if Zelophehad's daughters married outside their tribe, their land would become a source of dispute between the two tribes. So Moses stipulated that these daughters could only marry within their tribe, or else they would forfeit their claim to the land so as to avoid such disputes.

After all the battles the Israelites had to fight and the internal bickering they had to deal with, it seems this generation was ready to do things God's way for a change. The book of Numbers comes to a close with Zelophehad's daughters agreeing to this conflict-preventing stipulation, an act that provided great hope for the future peace and prosperity of the twelve tribes of Israel.

These women fought for a noble cause and won, because God was their advocate. Is there a noble cause that stirs your soul? Is there a social issue that concerns you or a group of people that prompts you to act on its behalf? Do you need an advocate to help you win a battle that you consider worthy of time and attention? If so, look no further. Psalm 37:3–6 tells us who our greatest Advocate is and how we gain His help:

Trust in the LORD and do good.
       Then you will live safely in the land and prosper.
Take delight in the LORD,
       and he will give you your heart's desires.

Commit everything you do to the LORD.
       Trust him, and he will help you.
He will make your innocence as clear as the dawn,
       and the justice of your cause will shine like the noonday sun.

If you are trusting in the Lord rather than in your own strength, then rest assured that victory is inevitable, girlfriend, for He is our almighty Advocate!

HOLDING HIS HAND

Do I have the courage and conviction to fight for causes that I consider just? Why or why not?

_____

_____

_____

_____

Do I consider God my adversary or my advocate? Why do I feel the way I do?

_____

_____

_____

What do my answers tell me about my belief in God? What do they tell me about my belief in myself as God's child?

_____

_____

_____

_____

Dear Lord,

Thank You for having a special place in Your heart for women and for being our Advocate. Thank You for what You did for Zelophehad's daughters and all of Your daughters since then. You have given us many blessings and opportunities to glorify You. May we always be good stewards of these gifts. Amen.

COMPLETELY
Loved BY...
OUR COMMANDER
IN CHIEF

Daily reading: Judges 4:1–5:31

Key passage: One day [Deborah] sent for Barak son of Abinoam.... She said to him, "This is what the LORD, the God of Israel, commands you: Assemble ten thousand warriors from the tribes of Naphtali and Zebulun at Mount Tabor. I will lure Sisera, commander of Jabin's army, along with his chariots and warriors, to the Kishon River. There I will give you victory over him."

Barak told her, "I will go, but only if you go with me!"

"Very well," she replied, "I will go with you. But since you have made this choice, you will receive no honor. For the LORD's victory over Sisera will be at the hands of a woman." (Judges 4:6–9)

Decorating the highways of my home state are signs that read Don't Mess with Texas. Of course, these signs are intended to discourage littering. But if there were signs marking the roads of God's Promised Land of Canaan (later called Israel), they would probably read, Don't Mess with My People!

God will do whatever it takes to defend His people and to defeat their enemies. In this particular instance, God chose women to do the job. Since women rulers weren't the norm in Israel, Deborah may have had the role of prophetess and judge because of a shortage of willing and able men. Sisera's troops with their nine hundred chariots had oppressed God's people long enough, so the Lord commanded Deborah to challenge Barak to lead the way in this battle.

Although Barak was willing to go, his insistence that Deborah accompany him implies that he did not have faith in *his* God, but rather in *Deborah's* God. Deborah's presence was his insurance policy against defeat. How sad that Barak did not have confidence in his heavenly Commander. Because of Barak's lack of faith, Deborah predicted that the honor of killing Sisera would belong to a woman.

Deborah's influence in this battle is undeniable. Not only did she call forth Barak as leader of the army, she also helped him rally the necessary troops. These hastily gathered soldiers may not have felt ready for Sisera's mighty army, but God told Deborah that this was indeed the time to strike. Rather than fret over their unfavorable odds, Deborah knew the Lord was a trustworthy and reliable commander. The soldiers would do as He instructed. Deborah announced that the Lord had already gone ahead of their army, and sure enough, they crushed their enemy in the battle. Only Sisera escaped.

Of course, a battle wasn't considered complete until the leaders were captured or killed. This is where another woman, Jael, comes onto the scene as one of the heroines of this showdown. She hospitably lured the frightened leader into her tent as a place of refuge, offering him nourishment, rest, and seclusion from his pursuers. Jael then proved herself to be (1) not as hospitable as she seemed, (2) very quick with a hammer and tent peg (she killed Sisera by pounding a tent peg into his temple), and (3) the fulfillment of Deborah's prediction that a woman would be credited for the victory.

With the death of Sisera, the victory was final. The Canaanites never posed a threat to the Israelites again. They may have started out yelling, "You want a piece of me?" But God had the final word. I can just imagine Him saying, "When you mess with My people, you mess with Me!"

God is always watching over us. He stands ready to lead us either into battle or away from battle, based on His sovereign knowledge. He is entirely trustworthy, as He always wins. Knowing that our God is willing and able to do whatever it takes to ensure our victory and protection should give us complete confidence in Him as our heavenly Father, our Bridegroom, and our Commander in Chief.

HOLDING HIS HAND

If God can equip and empower Deborah and Jael to give the Israelite army victory over their oppressors, can He equip and empower me for victory as well? Why or why not?

_____

_____

_____

_____

What are some of the biggest battles I face in life? How do they affect me?

_____

_____

_____

_____

Have I turned these battles over to Him and invited Him to be my Commander in Chief? Why or why not?

_____

_____

_____

_____

Sovereign God,

You never cease to amaze us with Your creative ways! You always find a way to lead Your people away from danger and oppression. Give us confidence that You are big enough and strong enough to protect us, even in the midst of our fiercest battles.

COMPLETELY
Loved BY...

OUR SUPERNATURAL DELIVERER

Daily reading: Exodus 1–2; 13:17–22; 14

Key passage: But Moses told the people, "Don't be afraid. Just stand where you are and watch the LORD rescue you. The Egyptians that you see today will never be seen again. The LORD himself will fight for you. You won't have to lift a finger in your defense!" (Exodus 14:13–14)

One of my first jobs as a young teen was to deliver products for our local Avon representative. I would sort the shipment of colorful nail polishes, lipsticks, and other cosmetics into little white bags, load a few at a time into my bicycle basket, and set out on my journey, getting a kick out of ringing people's doorbells and yelling, "Ding, dong! Avon calling!" just like on the commercials. My husband's first job was also as a delivery person. He rolled and rubber-banded the local newspaper every afternoon, throwing rolled papers at people's doorsteps throughout the neighborhood. In college, one of my friends became a driver for the United Parcel Service (UPS). Dressed in her brown shorts and hiking boots, she zipped all around town in her huge brown truck, delivering boxes and collecting signatures at every stop. Look in the want ads on any given day, and chances are that delivery people are needed somewhere in town.

God has also worked through the ages as a delivery person of sorts, although His job is far more complex and challenging than delivering cosmetics, newspapers, or packages. God has been, and will always be, a supernatural Deliverer of His people.

In today's reading, we see God deliver one particular individual, Moses, from infanticide. Pharaoh insisted that all Hebrew male babies be killed by the midwives delivering them, but the midwives feared God and let them live. So Pharaoh declared that all Jewish boys be thrown into the Nile River upon their birth. During this time, a baby boy was born to a Hebrew woman. Because she feared for his life, she placed her baby boy into a basket and sent him floating down the Nile, hoping God would deliver him into safe hands. Indeed, God placed him in Pharaoh's daughter's hands, and she adopted him and named him Moses, (meaning "I drew him out of the water").

It may seem ironic or coincidental, but I call it a God thing that He delivered Moses *from* the water, then years later He delivered His people *through* the water. And this was no small feat. The logistics of delivering cosmetics, newspapers, or packages are miniscule in comparison to delivering thousands of men, women, children, animals, and all of their possessions (not to mention the possessions they plundered from the Egyptians upon their departure) through an enormous body of water while their furious enemies were in hot pursuit. I imagine that Pharaoh's army assumed they had the Israelites cornered with the desert behind them and the Red Sea in front of them. They had no idea that the Israelites were about to take a hike, while the Egyptian horses, chariots, and soldiers were about to take a swim.

The Lord assured His people of His presence by appearing before them as a pillar of cloud to guide them in the daytime and a pillar of fire to guide them by night (Exodus 13:21). But interestingly, in Exodus 14:19–20, the pillar moved. It was no longer in front of the Israelites, guiding them. Where did it go? Behind them, to protect them from the pursuing army. In fact, the cloud that separated them brought darkness to the Egyptians while providing light to the Israelites! How cool is that?

There may be times you feel stuck between a desert of desperation and an ocean of fear, with seemingly no way around, or out of, your situation. But guess what? God has a plan to deliver you *through* your troubles. Although unseen by your human eyes, He is there, eager to lead you through these tough times to a more peaceful season. If you can't sense His presence in front of you, maybe, as with the Israelites, He has moved to the rear. If you'll listen carefully, you'll hear Him saying, "I've got your back, my beloved bride!"

Perhaps what you are facing is not a Red Sea, where your blood is in danger of being spilled by an enemy. Maybe your situation is more like a blue sea of depression and sadness that seems to be draining the life out of you, a green sea of envy over what others have and you simply cannot afford, or a black sea of sickness looming large over your body or the body of a loved one. Regardless of what circumstances you face, God is ever present, and eager to be your supernatural Deliverer. Trust Him.

HOLDING HIS HAND

Do I believe that God is still in the delivery business? Why or why not, and what proof do I have?

What does today's passage teach me about God's ability to protect me and deliver me from my seen and unseen enemies? Do I trust Him to work in my own life in such supernatural ways?

What friend or family member do I know who may feel caught between a desert of desperation and an ocean of fear? How can I encourage him or her with the knowledge that God is willing and able to deliver us through our troubles?

_____

_____

_____

Dearest Lord God,

How small our problems seem in comparison to those of the Israelites as they made their exodus out of Egypt, yet You still care! Forgive us for losing sight of how powerful You are to save Your people, whether from the enormous threat of annihilation or from the little annoyances of life. Help us put our trust in You to deliver us through our troubles, and show us how to help others put their trust in You as well. In Jesus' name. Amen.

COMPLETELY *Loved* BY...

OUR LAW GIVER

Daily reading: Exodus 19:1–20:20

Key passage: And they said to Moses, "You tell us what God says, and we will listen. But don't let God speak directly to us. If he does, we will die!"

"Don't be afraid," Moses said, "for God has come in this way to show you his awesome power. From now on, let your fear of him keep you from sinning!" (Exodus 20:19–20)

---

*I*t's often a bad idea to send a child to do a parent's job. On occasion I've asked my daughter to inform my son that it's time to turn off the video games and tend to his chores. Matthew's response? Well, let's just say that it's been a far cry from the "Yes ma'am" that I would have expected had I delivered the message personally. I've also sent my son to Erin's room to tell her it's time to get off the phone and take care of her homework, which has resulted in something resembling a catfight the moment he walked across the threshold. If I had just stuck my own head in rather than sending Matthew, Erin would have been off the phone in seconds flat for fear that her privileges would be revoked.

Siblings don't usually fear one another, but they do fear their parents. I'm not talking about the kind of fear that makes them afraid of me, but rather the kind of fear that leads them to respect and obey me. This is the kind of fear we are to have of God as well. Although He is very loving and approachable, He also has a right to expect our obedience.

Today's reading is an often-misunderstood passage of Scripture in that God appears distant and aloof as He gives Moses the Law for His people to live by. However, the simple fact that He came to Mount Sinai to make His will known to His people makes this an incredibly intimate encounter.

Why would God go to such great lengths to communicate with the nation of Israel? Because He loved them passionately and wanted to make Himself known to them. When we stop to consider how He could have chosen to communicate the Ten Commandments, we realize that His chosen method was extraordinarily personal. Rather than quietly inspire Moses one night in his tent while everyone else was sleeping, God made a big production so that the people would know that these were God's laws, not just Moses's. Speaking to Moses alone and then sending him to inform the people could have perhaps resulted in the same rebellion that my children have engaged in with one another. I can just hear the squabbling now...

Moses: "You should honor your father and mother!"
Israelites: "God didn't really say that! You made that up!"
Moses: "Thou shalt not steal!"
Israelites: "Oh yeah, and what are you going to do about it?"
Moses: "Do not commit adultery!"
Israelites: "You are not the boss of me!"

God didn't want to take a chance that the Israelites would doubt Moses. He knew they needed to hear His commands coming from His own mouth in order for obedience to be inspired. The Lord explained to Moses, "I am going to come to you in a thick cloud so the people themselves can hear me as I speak to you. Then they will always have confidence in you" (Exodus 19:9).

You may wonder why God didn't come down and speak to the nation face to face. Why did He appear in a thick cloud? Why couldn't anyone besides Moses and Aaron be permitted to cross the boundary and ascend the mountain to behold the Lord? God is impressing upon the people that there is a boundary between humans and the divine, and that we need a mediator to serve as a go-between to connect imperfect people with such a perfect God. During the Old Testament era, Moses and the priests and prophets served as mediators between the people and God. In the New Testament era and in contemporary times, Jesus Christ serves as that mediator. Because the perfect Son of God paid the ultimate price of death on a cross to remove all of our sin—once for all—we can approach God on our own, with confidence (see Hebrews 4:14–16).

Finally, why did God feel that we needed laws in the first place? Aren't they really just a stumbling block that makes us fall into temptation and sin? Absolutely not. The Law is like a fence surrounding a playground. We can play freely inside the boundary, but when we climb over it and run out into the street, that's when we're in great danger of being hurt. God's laws are intended to give us freedom while keeping us from danger and self-destruction. Not just that, but they are also designed to ultimately benefit and bless us.

Think about it. The first three laws (serving no other gods, avoiding idols, and avoiding the misuse of His name) keep us in right relationship with God. Who doesn't want and need that? The next law (observing the Sabbath day) allows us to rest from our labor and to worship our Lord. What a welcome opportunity! Finally, the last six laws (honoring our parents and avoiding murder, adultery, theft, lying, and jealousy) keep us in right relationship with society, not to mention keeping us out of jail!

Who can complain about God directing us in such a way, for His laws also protect us from having these grievances and crimes committed against us. They are the moral fabric of our society, and they are blessings, not burdens. Trying to go through life without these laws would be like trying to play a board game without written instructions. Soon everyone would be making up their own rules, fussing and fighting, and no one would be having any fun. But with these instructions, we can enjoy spiritual health and happiness in our relationships with God, ourselves, and each other.

HOLDING HIS HAND

What does today's reading teach me about how God feels toward His people?

_____

_____

_____

What have my feelings been toward the Ten Commandments in the past? Although they may feel like a burden when I fail to obey them, have I also recognized them as blessings? Why or why not?

_____

_____

_____

Have my feelings changed at all as a result of today's reading? If so, how?

_____

_____

_____

Sovereign Lord,

Just as a father wants to protect his children and inspire them toward greatness, You also desire to do the same for us. Thank You for loving us enough to descend from Your throne and provide Moses with the laws that You would have us live by even today. Write these laws on the tablets of our hearts and make them our delight in order that we can delight You with our respectful obedience. Amen.

COMPLETELY

Loved BY...

OUR SOURCE
OF OPTIMISM

Daily reading: Numbers 13–14

Key passage: But Caleb tried to encourage the people as they stood before Moses. "Let's go at once to take the land," he said. "We can certainly conquer it!"

But the other men who had explored the land with him answered, "We can't go up against them! They are stronger than we are!" So they spread discouraging reports about the land among the Israelites: "The land we explored will swallow up any who go to live there. All the people we saw were huge. We even saw giants there, the descendants of Anak. We felt like grasshoppers next to them, and that's what we looked like to them!" (Numbers 13:30–33)

---

*I*magine watching the drama of the Israelites unfold. In Exodus, God delivers Israel from Egyptian slavery through a series of ten plagues. He miraculously parts the Red Sea, then releases the walls of water to drown their enemies. He leads the Israelites on their freedom journey with a pillar of cloud by day and a pillar of fire by night. He rains manna down from heaven to fill their empty bellies and brings forth water from a rock to quench their thirst. Over and over He proves that there's nothing He won't do to protect and provide for His chosen people.

Then He positions them on the outskirts of a prime piece of real estate, a bountiful land "flowing with milk and honey" (Numbers 13:27) and bearing clusters of grapes so large that they have to be carried on a pole by two men (see verse 23)! I've shopped in a lot of farmers' markets, and never have I seen grapes so big that I had to have help carrying them. The land must have been a horticultural paradise. And it was promised to them. It's like God set a luscious banquet table in their honor and said, "Feel free to dig in, guys! Don't be shy!" All they had to do was go in and stake their claim to the land that God was granting them.

Unfortunately, it didn't seem so simple to any of the Israelites, with the exception of an optimistic handful—particularly Caleb, Joshua, Moses, and Aaron. To everyone else, victory seemed impossible. In fact, they cried all night, wishing they had stayed in Egypt, and even plotting how they could return (see Numbers 14:1–4). Didn't they remember how they were in slavery there? Didn't they remember who they were and whose they were? They were God's chosen people! Yet they didn't have confidence in God, even after all He had done to prove Himself. Where did this lack of confidence lead them? Into rebellion, discouragement, and eventually death.

Rather than seeing God as more mighty and powerful than all of the Amorites put together, the Israelites considered themselves as "grasshoppers" in comparison. Their eyes were focused on the creation rather than the Creator, and it evoked fear and terror in their hearts. It's as if they were looking in a carnival fun-house mirror that distorted their image and made them appear much smaller than they really were. If only they could have seen themselves through God's eyes!

Caleb and Joshua were the only two of the twelve spies who said, "Yeah! We can take 'em! Come on!" Their valiant optimism reminds us that there are definitely rewards for having faith. Out of the entire nation, they were the only two whom God allowed to take possession of the Promised Land over forty years later. I'm sure Caleb and Joshua were tempted at times during those years to say, "See! I told you so! We could have taken them, but oh, no! You were too chicken!" (Or maybe they would have said, "You were too grasshopper!")

Sometimes challenges we face seem much bigger than they really are. But do you realize that as the bride of Christ, you can do anything God calls you to do? You can go wherever God calls you to go. You can claim anything God tells you is yours. You can face any giants and be victorious.

For example, lots of people told me that trying to get a book published would be like a tiny grain of sand getting noticed on an entire continent of beach. The message seemed to be, "Don't waste your time. It's not going to happen for you." But every time I got yet another rejection letter in the mail, I sensed God reminding me, "You only need one yes, Shannon! Keep trying! I'm on your side!" So I remained optimistic, until I finally got my yes. Some of my daughter's friends questioned her sanity when she announced that she was going to raise over four thousand dollars to go on a one-month mission trip to Romania. The looks on their faces told Erin what they were thinking; *But you can't do that! You're only fourteen!* Yet, she raised every penny and spent a month loving on little Romanian orphans last summer. When my friend Stacy got the news that she'd have to fight the giant of breast cancer, doctors didn't hold out much hope for survival. But Stacy had two young children to raise, and she wasn't going down without a fight. She remained optimistic about the Great Physician's healing powers. She's now been cancer free for over three years.

Nothing is impossible with God, girlfriend! Nothing. Because of Him, you are a giant and the problems you face are mere grasshoppers. Boldly go wherever God calls you to go and fight the battles that God calls you to fight. He is the source of your optimism, and He'll never be in short supply!

HOLDING HIS HAND

Are there any challenges in my life that seem too big for me to conquer? If so, have I been looking at them through my own eyes or through God's eyes?

What will my life be like if I do not conquer these challenges? How will I feel about myself? about my relationship with God?

_____

_____

_____

If I fight this battle and win, what will my life be like? How will I feel about myself? about my relationship with God?

_____

_____

_____

Based on my answers, what are some practical steps of obedience I can take in order to express my faith and optimism?

_____

_____

_____

> *Faithful God,*
>
> *No challenge is too great for You. No task is too hard for You. No dream is too big for You to fulfill. Give me the faith to trust in Your strength wholeheartedly and give me an optimistic point of view when facing every situation in life.*

COMPLETELY

Loved BY...

OUR FEARLESS LEADER

Daily reading: Joshua 5:13–6:27

Key passage: When the people heard the sound of the horns, they shouted as loud as they could. Suddenly, the walls of Jericho collapsed, and the Israelites charged straight into the city from every side and captured it. They completely destroyed everything in it—men and women, young and old, cattle, sheep, donkeys—everything.... So the LORD was with Joshua, and his name became famous throughout the land. (Joshua 6:20–21, 27)

---

*I*f someone were to ask you, "Who won the battle at Jericho?" how would you respond? Would you say, "Joshua?" Indeed, most of us would. Perhaps you even sang the song in Sunday school, "Joshua fought the battle of Jericho, Jericho, Jericho; Joshua fought the battle of Jericho, and the walls came tumbling down!"

While I'm not looking to be nitpicky here, I want to clarify that Joshua didn't win that battle. Scripture makes it clear that Joshua wasn't the fearless leader, but merely a fearless follower. In Joshua 6:2, the Lord said, "I have given you Jericho, its king, and all its mighty warriors." The Lord didn't say,

"I *will* give you Jericho," as if it were something that would happen in the future. He said, "I *have given* you Jericho," implying that the battle had already been fought and won in the spiritual realm. All that was left for Joshua and the Israelites to do was to go through the motions that God required of them to demonstrate their faith in the almighty God's leadership.

I can imagine that the Israelites were tempted to question Joshua's sanity when he proposed the game plan. Perhaps some even inquired, "You want us to do what? March around the walls silently while priests blow rams' horns? Every day for a week? Then march around seven times on the seventh day and yell at the top of our lungs? And this is going to make the walls fall down?" After all, they knew those walls were probably made of limestone, not lime Jell-O.

This plan would have to seem rather far-fetched to even the simplest of minds. But because God had already fought the battle and given Jericho to Joshua, it wouldn't have mattered if He'd asked them to do the Hokey Pokey in pink pajamas. Those walls were coming down as long as the people obeyed the Lord's instruction.

Why was God determined to hand Jericho over to the Israelites? This was their first conquest in the land of Canaan. What you read about today is a holy parade of sorts. Who was the parade in honor of? God! The ark of the covenant that the Israelites carried was a symbol of God's presence. And notice the emphasis on the number seven. Seven priests were instructed to walk ahead of the ark blowing seven rams' horns. Victory would only come on the seventh day after marching around the city seven times. The number seven indicates divine perfection or completeness.[1] After forty years of the Israelites' whining, "How many more miles to the Promised Land?" this holy parade seems to be God's way of saying, "We're finally here, kids!"

There are many times in our lives when we need a fearless leader we can follow. I find myself frequently praying to ask God to go before me into a situation to ensure victory and success. *Lord, go before us as we travel and smooth out any rough spots in the road. Go before this proposal and give this idea favor. Go before me as I approach this person to ask forgiveness.* When God goes ahead of me, whom or what have I to fear? Absolutely no one and nothing. My God tears down walls. He renders my enemies helpless. He melts hearts. He moves heaven and earth to get my attention and bestow His favor on me. I can't lose when I follow my Fearless Leader.

Perhaps you need a fearless leader to follow these days. Whether you have an important job interview coming up, a relationship that needs reconciling, or a sinful habit that you are battling, don't try to do such things in your own strength. You have a Fearless Leader, so simply play the role of fearless follower, as Joshua did. Your heavenly Bridegroom is happy to lead you into your own promised land of victory. Simply obey His instructions, regardless of how random they may seem at the time. Then someday you will look back and see only the rubble that remains from the challenging walls that God has broken down for you.

HOLDING HIS HAND

What walls am I facing that need to be broken down by my Fearless Leader?

_____

_____

_____

Are there specific things that I sense God wants me to do in order to show my faith in His leadership?

_____

_____

_____

Do I believe that God will give me victory in every situation when I follow Him? Why or why not?

_____

_____

_____

Fearless Lord,

Thank You for going before me in every situation. Give me the strength and courage to be a fearless follower, knowing that You are fully trustworthy. And please tear down any walls that separate me from You. In Jesus' name. Amen.

COMPLETELY
Loved BY...
OUR EVER-PRESENT
PROTECTOR

Daily reading: Genesis 28:10–22; 35:1–15

Key passage: As he slept, he dreamed of a stairway that reached from earth to heaven. And he saw the angels of God going up and down on it.

At the top of the stairway stood the LORD, and he said, "I am the LORD, the God of your grandfather Abraham and the God of your father, Isaac. The ground you are lying on belongs to you. I will give it to you and your descendants. Your descendants will be as numerous as the dust of the earth! They will cover the land from east to west and from north to south. All the families of the earth will be blessed through you and your descendants. What's more, I will be with you, and I will protect you wherever you go. I will someday bring you safely back to this land. I will be with you constantly until I have finished giving you everything I have promised." (Genesis 28:12–15)

What specific things did you inherit from your parents and grandparents? Perhaps you have your father's artistic flair or your mother's cheery disposition. Or maybe what you inherited from your relatives is more tangible, such as your grandfather's pocket watch or your grandmother's pearl necklace.

From my mother's side, I inherited the "Bailey cowlick." Everyone on that side of the family has a hairline that grows rather strangely compared to most people's, thus I've been fighting with my bangs every morning since childhood. From my father's side of the family, I inherited a set of Noritake china with a beautiful dogwood pattern. I'll never forget telling my grandmother when I was ten years old how much I loved her dogwood dishes. She responded by tugging me onto her lap and whispering to me softly, "I've put it in my will that when I die, I want you to have this china." That set of dishes is one of my most prized possessions.

In today's reading, Jacob receives a priceless inheritance. The promises God made to his grandfather Abraham, and then to his father, Isaac, God now gives to Jacob. God promises Jacob three things: he will own a particular parcel of land, he will have numerous descendants to dwell in that land, and all families on earth will be blessed through him. Not too shabby an inheritance, huh?

But with Jacob, God goes a step further. In Genesis 28:15, He says, "What's more, I will be with you, and I will protect you wherever you go. I will someday bring you safely back to this land. I will be with you constantly until I have finished giving you everything I have promised."

Why does God specifically promise to protect Jacob? Because Jacob needs it! His name means "deceiver," and he has certainly lived up to that reputation already. Before he came to Bethel the first time, he had deceived his blind father and ticked his big brother off royally by stealing both his birthright and his blessing. In fact, Jacob came to Bethel because he was running for his life, figuring that Esau was right behind him with spear in hand to take revenge. (For more about Jacob's deception of Esau, see the next devotional in the series, *Completely Forgiven*.)

Much happened in Jacob's life between his two visits to Bethel (see Genesis 28 and Genesis 35). Competitive wives pulled him in two different directions, making him a pawn in their baby-making game. His manipulative father-in-law took advantage of him at every turn, and his angry brothers-in-law stole from him. Jacob even wrestled all night with an angel of God and ended up walking with a limp. If anyone ever needed divine protection, Jacob did!

The Lord faithfully provided such protection, just as He had promised. In Genesis 35:3, we see Jacob proclaiming, "We are now going to Bethel, where I will build an altar to the God who answered my prayers when I was in distress. He has stayed with me wherever I have gone." Jacob establishes a stone memorial the first time he passes through Bethel, and he puts up another when he returns. Sandwiched between these two events is example after example of God's sovereign protection of Jacob. God was certainly with Jacob moment by moment and faithful to His promises.

The Lord's promise to be an ever-present protector applies to us as well. It's our inheritance as a child of God. Just as a father watches his precious daughter closely, or just as a husband carefully guards his wife whenever he senses danger, our heavenly Father and Bridegroom never loses sight of us and goes to great lengths to put a hedge of protection around our minds, bodies, hearts, and souls.

Do you need protection? Are there people in your life who take aim at you with their explosive outbursts? Is poverty lurking at your door? Does fear or depression seem to have a tight grip on you? Or are you, like me, your own worst enemy at times, engaging in self-defeating behaviors and negative thought patterns? Regardless of what you need protection from, I encourage you to look up and recognize that you, like Jacob, have a mighty Protector watching over you. He won't let any of these things overtake you when you run to Him for cover, because remember, you are not just anybody. You are His chosen. You are His beloved bride.

HOLDING HIS HAND

Are there physical or spiritual places in my life where I have sensed God's promise of protection?

How can I return to that place and establish a memorial of praise for God's protection? How can I show my gratitude to Him?

_____

_____

_____

What is the Lord's protection based on, and why does this matter?

_____

_____

_____

> *Our Ever-Present Protector,*
>
> *Help me to recognize my priceless inheritance as Your precious child and Your chosen bride. Remind me that You protect Your own out of love and concern for us. And thank You that Your protection isn't based on my worthiness, but on Your goodness.*

COMPLETELY
Loved BY...
OUR ASSURANCE

Daily reading: Judges 6:1–8:21

Key passage: Then Gideon said to God, "If you are truly going to use me to rescue Israel as you promised, prove it to me in this way. I will put some wool on the threshing floor tonight. If the fleece is wet with dew in the morning but the ground is dry, then I will know that you are going to help me rescue Israel as you promised." And it happened just that way. When Gideon got up the next morning, he squeezed the fleece and wrung out a whole bowlful of water.

Then Gideon said to God, "Please don't be angry with me, but let me make one more request. This time let the fleece remain dry while the ground around it is wet with dew." So that night God did as Gideon asked. The fleece was dry in the morning, but the ground was covered with dew. (Judges 6:36–40)

What does it take to turn a coward into a courageous, cold-blooded killer? In Gideon's case, a great deal of divine assurance.

The scene opens with him using the bottom of a winepress as a threshing floor so he can hide the wheat (and himself) from the marauding Midianites. An angel of the Lord appears to him and says, "Mighty hero, the LORD is with you!" (Judges 6:12). Talk about hyperbole! Of course, the Lord is with Gideon, but Gideon is no mighty hero, not yet anyway. This angel appears to be assigning him this role rather than describing a role he has already played. In fact, as the story pans out, this angel appears to be the Lord Himself, and His words are prophetic.

Gideon questions why the Midianites are treating the Israelites like redheaded stepchildren. God replies, "Go with the strength you have and rescue Israel from the Midianites. I am sending you!" (Judges 6:14).

But Gideon's not so sure about this idea. His family comes from the weakest tribe of Manasseh, and he is likely the youngest and smallest (or the "least," as he says in verse 15) of the whole group. He's probably thinking, *Oh, boy. I should have eaten my Wheaties this morning!* I picture Gideon as a Napoleon Dynamite sort of character, scratching his head and wondering out loud, "Are you sure you've got the right guy, God?"

Even with God's assurance that He will be with him as he attacks the enemy, Gideon is likely thinking, *I'd better get a surefire sign on this or else I'm Midianite mincemeat!* He prepares a sizable offering and presents it to the Lord. When the offering is consumed, Gideon still doesn't seem confident about what God has said. Instead, Gideon fears death because seeing the Lord face to face usually renders a person lifeless. I can just imagine God replying, "Uh, Gideon. I just told you that I'm making you a mighty hero. You can't be a hero if you are dead!"

Gideon's first assignment is to tear down the altar to Baal and the Asherah pole so that sacrifices can no longer be made to these false gods. But he sets about this task at night, fearful of getting caught. He gets caught anyway, and he lets his daddy plead his case with the angry mob. Then the Spirit of the Lord comes upon Gideon (Judges 6:34), and we expect to see some big changes, but Gideon still needs more assurance.

He throws out a fleece and wants God to make it wet with dew while keeping the ground around it dry. God complies. But then Gideon wants God to do the opposite—make the ground wet while keeping the fleece dry. God again demonstrates His patience and gives Gideon an added measure of assurance. This gets Gideon up for battle early the next morning. But God tells him to send all of the cowardly soldiers home, which reduces the army by another two-thirds...and then God weeds out all but three hundred remaining soldiers. Gideon now has less than 1 percent of his original army left. If the odds for victory seemed less than promising before, surely they seem next to impossible now.

What does God do? I love this about God! He gives Gideon *yet another* confirmation, allowing him to overhear two enemy soldiers discussing a dream. Realizing this dream was far more than just coincidence, Gideon falls to the ground in worship of the God who sees his fearful heart, yet supplies him with an even greater measure of faith. Now Gideon is ready for battle, and victory comes swiftly. He goes from zero to hero in record time.

What can we learn from God's response to Gideon? That God is more than willing to assure us that we understand Him correctly. We all face situations where we are somewhat apprehensive and want to make sure we've heard clearly from God. We don't want to act impulsively without a clear vision of what we are to do and how we are to do it. So sometimes we throw our own fleece out. When we do this out of faith that God wants to guide us, I believe He is inclined to give us the assurance we need.

What kind of fleece do you need to throw out to God these days? Is He prompting you to discuss a fresh idea with your team at work? Or send an updated résumé to a new company? Or make a call to someone you haven't been on good terms with lately? Is He prompting you to make a donation to a church or ministry that seems like a bigger sacrifice than what you are typically comfortable with? Or to share your testimony with a women's Bible study or youth group? What kind of sign would give you the confirmation you need in order to proceed?

A good place to seek confirmation is in God's Word. Sometimes when I'm facing a dilemma, a particular character or passage of Scripture will come to mind and I find my answers right there in the pages of the Bible. Other times, I will be reading my Bible and God will speak to me through the passage I'm scheduled to read that day. Keep in mind that just flipping through the Bible and opening it to any verse isn't a good way to get assurance from God about what you should do. You could come across verses like Matthew 27:5 where "Judas…hanged himself."

So, if you need confirmation, don't hesitate to ask for it. God doesn't want you to stumble around in the dark, wondering what He expects of you. He wants you to move forward with confidence, and He's more than willing to give you the assurance you need.

HOLDING HIS HAND

What do I sense that God may be prompting me to do that makes me a little apprehensive about whether or not I am hearing Him correctly?

_____

_____

_____

_____

Where does my hesitation come from? Fear of failure? Or genuine concern that I act in accordance with His will?

_____

_____

_____

_____

What sign can I ask God for in order to feel assured that I'm doing the right thing? How do I feel about asking for such a sign, and why do I feel the way I do?

_____

_____

_____

_____

Heavenly Father,

Thank You for being patient with our fears, even though we have no reason to fear with You looking after us so closely. We all face uncertain times in life, and we are so grateful that You are a God who longs to guide us into Your perfect will and give us the assurance we need. Grant us a heart of submission, a spirit of boldness, and complete confidence as we seek to obey You all the days of our lives.

COMPLETELY

Loved BY...

OUR MYSTERY REVEALER

Daily reading: Daniel 2; 4

Key passage: Daniel replied, "There are no wise men, enchanters, magicians, or fortune-tellers who can tell the king such things. But there is a God in heaven who reveals secrets, and he has shown King Nebuchadnezzar what will happen in the future. Now I will tell you your dream and the visions you saw as you lay on your bed.

"While Your Majesty was sleeping, you dreamed about coming events. The revealer of mysteries has shown you what is going to happen. And it is not because I am wiser than any living person that I know the secret of your dream, but because God wanted you to understand what you were thinking about." (Daniel 2:27–30)

---

*I*magine the ruler of your country saying, "Tell me about the dream I had last night as well as what it means, or kiss your life good-bye!" Talk about pressure! Leaping over the palace walls in a single bound would probably have seemed like a much easier request to Nebuchadnezzar's wise men than did this absurd expectation.

Indeed, we can sense their panic as they respond, "There isn't a man alive who can tell Your Majesty his dream! And no king, however great and powerful, has ever asked such a thing of any magician, enchanter, or astrologer! This is an impossible thing the king requires. No one except the gods can tell you your dream, and they do not live among people" (Daniel 2:10–11).

Daniel steps in and says that while *their* gods do not live among people, his God, the one, true God, certainly lives among His people and even communicates clearly with them. After Daniel goes on to correctly explain and interpret Nebuchadnezzar's dreams, the king proclaims to Daniel, "Truly, your God is the God of gods, the Lord over kings, a revealer of mysteries, for you have been able to reveal this secret" (Daniel 2:47).

Unfortunately, Nebuchadnezzar's knowledge of Daniel's God is limited to his head rather than his heart. He soon erects a golden image and demands that everyone worship the Babylonian government (we'll read more about this tomorrow), then arrogantly takes the credit away from God for all that has transpired in his kingdom. As Nebuchadnezzar proclaims, "Just look at this great city of Babylon! I, by my own mighty power, have built this beautiful city as my royal residence and as an expression of my royal splendor" (Daniel 4:30), God's judgment is already on its way.

Do you know how miserable you feel when you are stuck out in the rain, you're having a really bad hair day, or your nails are screaming for a manicure? Multiply all of those miseries times one hundred and maybe you can envision how the king must have felt as he was drenched with dew, his hair became as long as the feathers of an eagle, and his nails like the claws of a bird (see Daniel 4:33). Pride proved to be not so pretty on Nebuchadnezzar, and it's equally ugly on us.

What can we learn from this passage? That no ruler or king is over God. No one can try to steal His glory and not pay a high price. God is above all and far beyond our control. We must submit to His sovereignty and control and give Him all the glory, as Daniel did, if we are to receive His favor and His guidance.

Another lesson is that God desires to reveal Himself, His ways, and His mysteries to His people. Notice that even under great stress and pressure, Daniel did not resort to occult practices for answers to any of these mysteries to be revealed. He simply went to God in prayer, and God gave him the wisdom he sought. Why did God choose to do this? Because His glory was at stake. He wasn't about to take a backseat to the other gods being consulted in the matter, and He had a message that He wanted to communicate to Nebuchadnezzar.

Dreams explained. Mysteries revealed. God is greater than any dream interpreter we could ever imagine. In Matthew 7:7–8 He promises, "Keep on asking, and you will be given what you ask for. Keep on looking, and you will find. Keep on knocking, and the door will be opened. For everyone who asks, receives. Everyone who seeks, finds. And the door is opened to everyone who knocks." Yet how many times do people turn to other sources for answers? The Babylonians had their magicians, diviners, enchanters, conjurers, sorcerers, and astrologers. But today we have our fortune-tellers, tarot-card readers, horoscopes, Dear Abby columns, and Dr. Phil–type television shows. I'm certainly not likening Abigail Van Buren or Phil McGraw to false gods, but I find it interesting how often we turn to other things and other people besides our all-knowing God for the guidance we seek to make our lives work.

What mystery are you needing revealed? Do you wonder why your husband or your children act the way they do, or better yet, what you can do to help the situation? Are you puzzled by a challenge at work that seems unsolvable? Do you wonder what causes you to feel stressed, depressed, angry, or anxious much of the time? Are you wondering how you can make ends meet financially or how you can create a better life for yourself?

Remember to take these questions and concerns to God first. He knows the best answers to the mysteries of your life. He alone sees the big picture and has the perfect prescription for your situation. He is eager to show you things and give you insight that even the best of counselors might overlook. For indeed, He is our perfect Counselor, our greatest Advocate, and the Revealer of all mysteries.

HOLDING HIS HAND

When I am puzzled by or frustrated with a situation, where or to whom do I usually turn for guidance? Why?

_____

_____

_____

How often do I turn to God in prayer about a matter before turning to other sources? Do I consider Him the real expert when it comes to what is happening in my life? Why or why not?

_____

_____

_____

What mystery am I struggling with today? How can I seek the Lord's guidance in the matter?

_____

_____

_____

Almighty God,

Even though I may often be tempted to seek the help of others first, I thank You for always standing by to reveal the solutions to the mysteries in my life. I rejoice over Your supernatural wisdom and delight in the fact that You long to share Your wisdom with me. Show me what You would have me understand, and keep my pride from trying to rob You of the glory that is rightfully all Yours.

COMPLETELY
Loved BY...

OUR SOVEREIGN PROMOTER

Daily reading: Daniel 1; 3

Key passage: God gave these four young men an unusual aptitude for learning the literature and science of the time....

When the three-year training period ordered by the king was completed, the chief official brought all the young men to King Nebuchadnezzar. The king talked with each of them, and none of them impressed him as much as Daniel, [Shadrach, Meshach, and Abednego]. So they were appointed to his regular staff of advisers. In all matters requiring wisdom and balanced judgment, the king found the advice of these young men to be ten times better than that of all the magicians and enchanters in his entire kingdom." (Daniel 1:17–20)

$\mathcal{M}$ any years ago I had an annoying friend. Why did I find him annoying? Because every time we got together he would say, "Hey! I've got big news! I got another promotion at work!"

Don't get me wrong. I was glad that my friend was succeeding at his job.

But after about the fourth or fifth identical announcement within a few months, I began to wonder what was up. Was he forgetting he told me already? Sometimes I'd respond, "That's great, Rick, but you told that me already," to which he would retort, "No, this is a new promotion that just happened today!" Then I began to wonder, *Do they promote employees every time they smile?* I finally suspected that he was so starved for recognition that he was probably fabricating many of these promotions. Once I even joked, "Well, after all of the promotions you've gotten in the past six months, you must be president of the company by now!"

When it comes to job promotions, Shadrach, Meshach, and Abednego made their way to the top of the Babylonian totem pole very quickly. These three young men (along with Daniel) were chosen from the Israelite masses to come into the king's service. The want ad in Daniel 1:4 reads something like this:

MEN WANTED: Must be strong, healthy, good-looking, young, well versed in every branch of learning, gifted with knowledge and good sense, and have the poise needed to serve in the royal palace.

Shadrach, Meshach, and Abednego were the cream of the crop, and this was a job with plenty of perks and bennies, including gourmet food and fine wines. The only problem was that the person offering these delicacies, the king of Babylon, wasn't their ultimate boss. The God of Abraham, Isaac, and Jacob was also the God of Shadrach, Meshach, and Abednego, and they didn't want to defile themselves by eating things forbidden by Jewish customs and dietary laws (see Leviticus 11 and Deuteronomy 14). So they asked to be excused from the king's feasts in order to consume a diet of vegetables and water. Yummy.

I'm not so sure I could exercise as much will power. Pass up Beef Wellington for broccoli (without cheese sauce)? Give up cheesecake and chocolate in exchange for carrots and cauliflower? Turn down eggnog in favor of eggplant? That would be hard for me. I'm thankful modern-day Christians are not bound by ancient Jewish dietary laws! But to Shadrach, Meshach, and Abednego, the question of "what's for dinner?" wasn't just a matter of pleasing their taste buds, but a matter of pleasing God. To them, this was a clear-cut issue of submission and obedience to their heavenly King, not their earthly king.

Fortunately, they were shown favor by the king's official when their vegetarian diet gave them a healthier glow than the other, more gluttonous students. Not only did God give them a healthy glow, but He also gave them an extraordinary learning curve as they excelled in all kinds of subjects and languages. I find it fascinating that after four semesters of Spanish classes, all I can remember is *Hola!* (Hello!), *Hamburgesa, por favor!* (Hamburger, please!) and *Banos?* (Bathroom?). Most of us have a hard enough time mastering our native tongue, let alone multiple languages. Obviously, God was with these young men, and the king considered them "ten times better" than his other wise men (Daniel 1:20).

In yesterday's reading, you may have noticed at the close of chapter 2 that Shadrach, Meshach, and Abednego were promoted from servants to administrators over the entire province of Babylon (see Daniel 2:49). Thanks to the good word that Daniel put in for them, they became the king's new golden boys. They quickly climbed the corporate ladder and were flying high in the king's court.

But times change quickly. Next we see Nebuchadnezzar enraged at these guys. Why? He had egotistically created a gold statue and demanded that everyone bow down to worship it as a sign of their commitment and loyalty to the Babylonian government. But when the musical instruments gave the signal, every forehead in the land bowed down to the ground with the exception of three—Shadrach's, Meshach's, and Abednego's. (Daniel was out of town on official business.) So instead of giving them another promotion, the king hands these servants their pink slips, or more accurately, one-way tickets into a fiery furnace stoked extra hot for their arrival.

If you had to make a choice between a quick face plant at the sound of a trumpet or a quick trip into a blazing inferno, could you be so bold as Shadrach, Meshach, and Abednego? They loved the Lord far more than their own lives, and they refused to worship anything or anyone other than Him, regardless of the cost. They nobly made their fearless declaration in Daniel

3:16–18: "O Nebuchadnezzar, we do not need to defend ourselves before you. If we are thrown into the blazing furnace, the God whom we serve is able to save us. He will rescue us from your power, Your Majesty. But even if he doesn't, Your Majesty can be sure that we will never serve your gods or worship the gold statue you have set up."

But even if he doesn't—can you imagine braver words than these? These men were willing to go into that fiery furnace for no other reason than to say, "We work for God alone, and we'll die proving it!" Now that's loyalty. So what do Shadrach, Meshach, and Abednego receive for their bravery and loyalty? A major miracle. They frolic around in the flames with an angel as if they were in a garden sprinkler on a warm summer day, then they walk out unharmed without even smelling like smoke!

As a result, God gets the first promotion, as King Nebuchadnezzar declares that anyone who speaks against the God of Shadrach, Meshach, and Abednego will be torn limb from limb (see Daniel 3:29). Then these three brave men get the next promotion, as they are moved into an even higher office in Babylon (see Daniel 3:30). I can only imagine the promotion that awaited them in heaven upon their arrival.

What about you? What kind of promotion are you looking for? Are you willing to compromise your personal holiness to please an earthly boss, or do you have your heavenly Boss's agenda in mind? Remain committed to the Lord Jesus Christ, and you can bet that more and more spiritual promotions await you. Simply seek to serve God with all of your heart and feel His favor upon you.

HOLDING HIS HAND

Am I as committed to personal holiness as Shadrach, Meshach, and Abednego? Why or why not?

Do I believe that God bestows favor, honor, and even promotions on those who are loyal to Him? Why do I believe the way I do?

_____

_____

_____

What kind of spiritual promotion might God want to give me? What special responsibilities do I hope to assume as His chosen bride?

_____

_____

_____

Lord Jesus,

Thank You for willingly dying for us, descending into the depths of a fiery furnace called hell just to cancel our reservation so that we can spend eternity in heaven with You. Help us to live a life worthy of our calling as the bride of Christ, and to trust You entirely to promote us to the next level, and the next, and the next. In Your most holy and precious name we pray. Amen.

COMPLETELY

Loved BY...

OUR LORD OVER
ALL CREATION

Daily reading: Jonah 1–4

Key passage: Then the sailors picked Jonah up and threw him into the raging sea, and the storm stopped at once! The sailors were awestruck by the LORD's great power, and they offered him a sacrifice and vowed to serve him.

Now the LORD had arranged for a great fish to swallow Jonah. And Jonah was inside the fish for three days and three nights. (Jonah 1:15–17)

I wasn't intending to eavesdrop, but the store was small and their voices were growing louder. A husband and wife were having a disagreement, and it was quickly becoming public knowledge what they were fussing about. She wanted to buy a new dress for a special occasion, but the price was beyond their budget. "This is a special day, and I want to look my best!" she whined.

"But you are missing the point, dear! I don't care how good you look in it, we simply can't afford it!" her husband insisted. He went on to jokingly remind her that since the credit card was in his wallet instead of her purse, he would win this argument. She finally got the point, but I don't think she was too happy about it.

Most of us have missed the point at times. We look at things through our own lens and fail to see reality. Unfortunately, this happens frequently as we read the Bible, particularly the story of Jonah, which is no fish tale but a historical account of God's sovereignty, mercy, and divine protection. When we heard this story as kids, we may have believed that Jonah was the star of this show, or perhaps the big fish that swallowed him up, but in so doing we missed the point.

Jonah is simply God's chosen instrument to deliver a warning to the ungodly Assyrians living in Nineveh. The big fish is simply the protection that God provided Jonah as he tried to rebel against God's instructions. But again, God is the real star of this show, and every human, animal, plant, and aspect of nature in this story plays a supporting role to demonstrate just how great our Creator really is.

Consider the following verses to support this theory:

- "But as the ship was sailing along, suddenly *the LORD flung a powerful wind over the sea,* causing a violent storm that threatened to send them to the bottom" (1:4).
- "Then the sailors picked Jonah up and threw him into the raging sea, and *the storm stopped at once!* The sailors were awestruck by the LORD's great power" (1:15–16).
- "Now *the LORD had arranged for a great fish* to swallow Jonah" (1:17).
- "Then *the LORD ordered the fish to spit up Jonah* on the beach, and it did" (2:10).
- "And *the LORD God arranged for a leafy plant to grow there,* and soon it spread its broad leaves over Jonah's head, shading him from the sun" (4:6).
- "But *God also prepared a worm!*" (4:7).
- "And as the sun grew hot, *God sent a scorching east wind* to blow on Jonah" (4:8).

In these seven passages we see the Lord controlling nature, from things as large and mighty as the wind and rain clouds, the waves of the sea, and a huge sea creature, to the smallest, most fragile things, such as a leafy plant and a lowly worm. Each of these aspects of nature willingly submits to God's control. He rules over all creation.

However, rather than controlling humans, God gives us free will. Jonah had a choice about whether to obey God. At first he disobeyed and tried to run, but he learned quickly that he couldn't outrun God. God often orchestrates the events and surroundings of our lives to inspire our obedience, but He never forces us to do something against our will. When Jonah finally decided to obey God, God proved Himself to be the God of second chances.

God also let the 120,000 people of Nineveh choose whether they would submit to His desires. Fortunately for them, they responded appropriately with fasting and mourning for their sin and with repentant hearts. As a result, they were spared God's discipline and destruction.

But there's an even greater point to this story, a point clearly spelled out by Jesus in Matthew 12:38–41:

> One day some teachers of religious law and Pharisees came to Jesus and said, "Teacher, we want you to show us a miraculous sign to prove that you are from God."
>
> But Jesus replied, "Only an evil, faithless generation would ask for a miraculous sign; but the only sign I will give them is the sign of the prophet Jonah. For as Jonah was in the belly of the great fish for three days and three nights, so I, the Son of Man, will be in the heart of the earth for three days and three nights. The people of Nineveh will rise up against this generation on judgment day and condemn it, because they repented at the preaching of Jonah. And now someone greater than Jonah is here—and you refuse to repent.

Do you, like the Pharisees, often look for a special sign that the Lord is truly God of the universe? Look no further. He's already given us plenty of proof in the Scriptures, so be careful not to miss the point. God is exactly who He claims He is—sovereign Lord of all creation, as well as the intimate Lover of our souls. There is no limit to what He can do, nor is there any limit to His lavish love for you.

HOLDING HIS HAND

Do I believe that God controls every aspect of the world He created? Why or why not?

_____

_____

_____

_____

God gives humans free will, unlike the nature that He controls. Why would He give us control over our own actions?

_____

_____

_____

_____

Do I consistently submit to His will for my life, or do I have a tendency to want to run and do my own thing as Jonah did? What is usually my reasoning for doing what I do?

_____

_____

_____

_____

How can I, like the city of Nineveh, demonstrate to God that I acknowledge His almighty power? Is there anything I need to repent of in order to submit to Him?

Most Powerful Lord,

We are so thankful that all of creation lies in the hands of such a loving and merciful God. We also appreciate that You do not force us to do anything, but instead diligently inspire us to pursue a right relationship with You. Help us not to overlook the main point of Your Word—that You love us beyond measure and have already moved heaven and earth to draw us closer to You.

COMPLETELY

Loved BY...

OUR COMPASSIONATE RESCUER

Daily reading: Genesis 18:16–19:38

Key passage: The next morning Abraham was up early and hurried out to the place where he had stood in the LORD's presence. He looked out across the plain to Sodom and Gomorrah and saw columns of smoke and fumes, as from a furnace, rising from the cities there. But God had listened to Abraham's request and kept Lot safe, removing him from the disaster that engulfed the cities on the plain. (Genesis 19:27–29)

God just seems so angry and harsh," said the young woman sitting next to me on the airplane. We were discussing the class in major world religions that she was taking at a junior college. When I asked what gave her such an impression of God, she quoted portions of today's Bible story, saying that she could never imagine Buddha or Allah raining down burning sulfur in judgment of a city.

This is another passage of Scripture where people often miss the point. The reality is that neither Buddha nor Allah—nor any other god—offers humanity the free gift of grace. In every religion other than Christianity, salvation must be earned, and there is no clear-cut way to determine if your works are ever good enough to earn it. Only God extends the assurance of salvation to His beloved—salvation based entirely on the grace He freely extends. So rather than focus on the destruction of Sodom and Gomorrah, which is happening in the background of the story, shift your attention to what is going on in the forefront—the bold prayers of a concerned uncle and the Lord's compassionate rescue of his nephew's family.

Before we dive deeper into the story, take a moment to imagine how moved a husband is by his wife's earnest plea. He loves her. He cherishes her. And so he listens when she speaks and tries to respond positively when she asks for a favor. As the father of the nation of Israel (Genesis 12:7), Abraham was the first member of the chosen bride of Christ. When he prayed, God listened. Even in the opening of this passage, we see God asking (Himself, no doubt, for who else would He ask?), "Should I hide my plan from Abraham?" (Genesis 18:17). In other words, God is saying, "If Abraham is my chosen beloved, I should make my business known to him!" And so He tells Abraham of His plans to pass judgment on a city reeking with rebellion and evil.

At this revelation, Abraham's intercession skills kick into high gear. He approaches God and says, "Will you destroy both innocent and guilty alike? Suppose you find fifty innocent people there within the city?"... What about forty?... Okay, suppose you find thirty?... even twenty?... Well, what about ten? (see Genesis 18:23–32). Of course, Abraham is really concerned about his nephew, Lot, and his family of four. And even though He cannot find even ten righteous people in the cities of Sodom and Gomorrah, God demonstrates His compassion and agrees to rescue Lot's family of four.

Why did God rescue Lot? I doubt it was because of Lot's righteousness, based on his offering his virgin daughters to some men who wanted to have sex not to mention the sexual relations his daughters have with him when he's in a drunken stupor (Genesis 19:8, 33–36). God rescued Lot's family because Abraham prayed. "But God had listened to Abraham's request and kept Lot safe, removing him from the disaster that engulfed the cities on the plain" (Genesis 19:29). Lot and his family were spared, in spite of his corrupt character. What a compassionate Rescuer we serve!

Regardless of what sin or danger you may find yourself entrenched in, our God is slow to anger, abounding in love, and eager to save you, whether from yourself, other people, or the things that corrupt your character. Not only that, God also listens to your prayers of intercession for those you care about. His answers to those prayers may not parallel your request, but rest assured that He does hear your prayers and responds in accordance with His divine will.

Are there people in your family or your circle of friends who need to be rescued from what is going on around them? Don't hesitate to boldly and confidently approach the Lord in prayer on their behalf. Remember, you are the bride of Christ, and your heavenly Bridegroom eagerly anticipates responding to your heartfelt requests.

HOLDING HIS HAND

When I think of the story of Sodom and Gomorrah, what aspects of God's character do I think of? Do I see Him as a harsh, angry judge or a compassionate rescuer?

_____

_____

_____

_____

Are there things or people (including myself) that I personally need to be rescued from? Have I approached God confidently with my cries for help?

_____

_____

_____

Are there others that I know of who need to be rescued by our compassionate God? Who are they, and how can I intercede with my heavenly Bridegroom on their behalf?

_____

_____

_____

_____

Compassionate Lord,

Although You despise evil, I know that You will never despise me. Thank You for listening intently to my prayers as a husband listens to his cherished bride. Show me who I need to intercede for and how You might desire to use me to play a role in their rescue. In Jesus' name. Amen.

COMPLETELY

Loved BY...

OUR SOURCE OF
INNER STRENGTH

Daily reading: 1 Samuel 17:32–51; 18:1–16; 19:1–10; 24; 26

Key passage: And [Saul] said to David, "You are a better man than I am, for you have repaid me good for evil. Yes, you have been wonderfully kind to me today, for when the LORD put me in a place where you could have killed me, you didn't do it. Who else would let his enemy get away when he had him in his power? May the LORD reward you well for the kindness you have shown me today. And now I realize that you are surely going to be king, and Israel will flourish under your rule." (1 Samuel 24:17–20)

When you think of David's strength, you likely envision the battle between David and Goliath and how a scrawny but stout-hearted shepherd boy knocked down an enormous giant of a man with only a sling and a stone. What an incredible display, not only of David's remarkable aim and amazing courage, but also of God's anointing on his life as a mighty warrior. However, as impressive as the story of David and Goliath is, I'm more impressed with the kind of strength David displayed in his ongoing struggle with King Saul.

Saul's jealousy of David more than likely began when David slaughtered Goliath, for Saul had wanted David to wear his armor in that battle. In those days, to wear the clothing of another was to be imbued with that person's essence, so if David had worn Saul's armor, Saul could have taken partial credit for David's victory.[1] Unfortunately for Saul, David felt his armor would be more of a hindrance than a help. Later, Saul's son Jonathan offered David his royal robe (a symbol of the Israelite kingdom), his tunic, and his armor (thus transferring his own status as heir apparent of the kingdom to David), and David accepted them without argument.[2] Surely this made Saul a little uncomfortable and even more jealous, and when the people began crediting David with ten times more battlefront casualties than Saul, it sent him into a murderous rage. Saul tried repeatedly to pin David to the wall with a spear. He sent David to the front lines of battle, hoping he'd be killed. Saul assembled an army of thousands of trained soldiers to hunt David down and snuff him out, all to no avail.

You'd think that after all these attempts, David would have felt justified in retaliating, right? *What goes around, comes around! Don't dish it out if you can't take it, Saul! An eye for an eye, a tooth for a tooth!* Even David's army was eager to get even with Saul, but David wouldn't hear of it. Why? Because David knew that God had anointed Saul to serve as king of Israel. God had anointed David as well, but David was determined that he would become king as a result of God's hand, not as a result of having his own hands tainted with Saul's blood.

Of course, this isn't to say that David didn't have multiple chances to kill Saul. But rather than cut off Saul's unsuspecting head in a cave, David settled for a corner of the king's robe. Rather than pin Saul to the ground with his own spear, David stole Saul's weapon and water jug. Regardless of how wrongly Saul treated him, David refused to reciprocate, and he went to great lengths to demonstrate that he considered Saul's life precious and sacred, even if Saul considered David's life worthless. David knew that two wrongs never make a right.

David's enormous self-restraint came from the Lord, and He can empower us with such inner strength as well. Are there times you want to bite off some-one's head for being so rude to you? Perhaps your husband? Your mother-in-law? Your boss? God can help you hold your tongue. Have you been tempted to smack your smart-alecky teenager for mouthing off one too many times? God can grant you all the self-control you need to avoid such a mistake. Of course, sometimes we can be our own worst enemy. Do you sometimes feel like eating or drinking yourself into oblivion to medicate your emotional pain? God can provide the will power you need to control your appetites and do what is most honoring to your body.

None of us has to be a slave to our anger or destructive desires, because our heavenly Bridegroom can shower us with the self-restraint we need to be the women of character we were created to be. We can consistently do the right thing, even if someone else is consistently doing the wrong things to us.

HOLDING HIS HAND

What part of today's Bible reading impresses me most about the strength that God gave David?

Do I rely on my own limited strength rather than looking to God for the self-control I need? If so, why?

Do I believe that God can help me act right, even when other people act wrong? Why or why not?

Most Awesome Lord,

Thank You for Your willingness to provide the self-restraint that we need in every situation. I admit that I don't always respond to other people in ways that bring You glory and honor. Help me not to stoop to another person's level, and show me how to treat others in such a way that they are inspired to a higher level. I ask this so that I can represent You well, Lord Jesus. Amen.

COMPLETELY
Loved BY...

OUR PROVIDENTIAL LORD

Daily reading: Ruth 1–4

Key passage: And again they wept together, and Orpah kissed her mother-in-law good-bye. But Ruth insisted on staying with Naomi. "See," Naomi said to her, "your sister-in-law has gone back to her people and to her gods. You should do the same."

But Ruth replied, "Don't ask me to leave you and turn back. I will go wherever you go and live wherever you live. Your people will be my people, and your God will be my God. I will die where you die and will be buried there. May the LORD punish me severely if I allow anything but death to separate us!" (Ruth 1:14–17)

Sandwiched between the books of Judges and 1 Samuel, we find the stirring story of Ruth, Naomi, and Boaz. In stark contrast to the surrounding stories about major events, warring countries, national judges, and royal kings, this book focuses on the plight of a single family. If you've ever operated a GPS navigation system in a car, you know that with several touches on the screen, you can go from an entire region to a specific city, then from the city to a particular street, and then from the street right down to a specific house. Think of the Bible doing exactly that, shifting its focus from the nation of Israel, to the tribe of Judah, and then to the individual family of Naomi and Elimelech.

The story goes something like this. Due to a famine in the land of Judah, Elimelech travels with his wife and two sons to a land called Moab. There he dies, leaving Naomi a widow in a foreign country. Naomi's two sons marry Moabite women, Orpah and Ruth. However, both sons die before Orpah and Ruth are able to bear any children. Not only is Naomi left a widow without any sons, but she has no hope of grandsons to take care of her in her old age. No wonder she wants to change her name to Mara, which means "bitter."

It makes the most sense for Naomi to return to Judah and for Orpah and Ruth to remain in Moab (for tribes tend to care for their own widows, but not necessarily for foreign widows). But Orpah and Ruth refuse to leave Naomi. All are torn. If Naomi stays, she is vulnerable. But if these two daughters-in-law leave their hometown and go to Judah as widows, they are the ones in vulnerable positions. Naomi tries to talk some sense into them, and Orpah returns to her mother's home, but Ruth is determined not to leave her beloved mother-in-law. She willingly abandons her home and her family to follow Naomi.

In case you don't recognize the magnitude of this act, let me spell it out for you—this is H-U-G-E. While you and I might move to another country without hesitation because we know our God is with us, things were very different in Ruth's culture. The power of the gods of a particular people-group was bound by their geographic location. The connection to one's family and land symbolized the connection to one's gods.[1] So Ruth was not only abandoning her homeland, family, and friends, she was also abandoning her own gods in order to follow Naomi's God, as demonstrated when she says to Naomi, "Your people will be my people, and your God will be my God" (Ruth 1:16).

After Naomi and Ruth arrive in Judah, God leads Ruth to glean in one field in particular, where she is able to gather enough food for herself and her mother-in-law. He also gives her favor in the eyes of the landowner, Boaz, who just happens to be a close relative of Elimelech's. Then God prompts Boaz to become Ruth's husband and redeem Elimelech's parcel of land (which had been sold to someone else since only children, not wives, were entitled to inherit land). In addition to a husband and a home, God gives Ruth children to carry on the family name and to inherit the family farm.

If there ever was a happily-ever-after story, this is it. But one might wonder about its significance, since God doesn't appear to be a central character. Don't lose sight of what is happening behind the scenes. God's providential hand is invisibly at work orchestrating events that will allow for the redemption and prosperity of both Naomi and Ruth. Why is God so concerned about these two widows? Besides the fact that God is concerned about *all* widows, God is demonstrating His divine providence here (a term that can be better understood by breaking it down into syllables—*provide*-ence). Why is God intent on providing for Ruth? Again, she had left her homeland, her family, and her gods to follow Naomi (and Naomi's God) back to Judah. Her loyalty does not go unnoticed by her Lord. Not only does He care for her physical needs and provide a husband and children for her, but He also gives her an exalted place in Hebrew history, including her in the direct lineage of Christ, as her first child would become the grandfather of David. When it comes to being the recipient of God's generous provision, a passionate commitment to Him is obviously more important than a genetic tie to the Hebrew people.

What about you? Are there certain provisions you need from God's generous hand? Do you have material needs, such as a safe home, a stocked pantry, a steady job, or a reliable car? Are you desirous of a husband, a child, or even more children? Or do you simply need God to provide you with a heart of gratitude for the house, job, husband, or children He's already given you?

Our providential Lord diligently cares for His beloved followers. Sometimes He will give you exactly what you ask for. Other times He gives you more of Himself to fill the void. Either way, trust that God knows what is best, petition Him with your prayers, then keep watch as He consistently cares for you.

HOLDING HIS HAND

What does today's reading tell me about God's concern not just for nations, but for individuals and families?

_____

_____

_____

Have I, like Ruth, abandoned my dependence on anyone or anything else in order to follow the God of Abraham, Isaac, and Jacob? Why or why not?

_____

_____

_____

What needs or desires have I been trying to fulfill on my own that I need to look to the Lord for? Write a brief prayer of surrender and petition.

_____

_____

_____

Most Generous God,

All that we have has come from Your hand, and all we ever hope to have is within Your power to grant us. Provide for us the things that we need in order to remain healthy and holy. Purify our motives for wanting the things we want. And most of all, help us to follow You wholeheartedly all the days of our lives.

COMPLETELY
Loved BY...
OUR SLATE CLEANER

Daily reading: Genesis 37; 42–45

Key passage: "I am Joseph!" he said to his brothers. "Is my father still
alive?" But his brothers were speechless! They were stunned to realize that
Joseph was standing there in front of them. "Come over here," he said.
So they came closer. And he said again, "I am Joseph, your brother whom
you sold into Egypt. But don't be angry with yourselves that you did this
to me, for God did it. He sent me here ahead of you to preserve your
lives." (Genesis 45:3–5)

Keeping score. Humans have been doing it since we were created.
Remember the words of Adam in Genesis 3:12? "But it was the
woman you gave me who brought me the fruit, and I ate it." In other words,
"It's her fault, Lord, not mine! The strike goes on her side of the scoreboard.
Don't count it against me."

Indeed, in the game of life, we're often tempted to chalk up everyone
else's fouls and strikes, just to make our own side of the scoreboard look more
impressive. But not Joseph. In the Me vs. My Brothers game, Joseph could
have easily taken the prize when it came to moral righteousness. The only

mark we can count against Joseph is for being proud and foolishly telling his brothers about his dreams that they would one day bow down to him (Genesis 37:5–11).

But our scoreboard would have to be pretty big to count all of his brothers' trespasses:

- Genesis 37:4: His brothers hate him and cannot speak a kind word to him. *Strike one!*
- Genesis 37:20: They plot to kill him and throw his dead body into a cistern. *Strike two!*
- Genesis 37:23–24: They strip him of his robe and throw him into an empty well. *Strike three!*
- Genesis 37:28: They sell him for twenty shekels, less than the price of a slave. *Strike four!*
- Genesis 37:31–33: They soak his robe in blood and lie to his father about his death. *Strike five!*

Joseph suffers some incredibly dark days during his captivity in Egypt (more about this in tomorrow's reading). Humanly speaking, he has every right to keep score of all of his brothers' sins against him and to expect that they would owe him big time once he caught up with them. However, Joseph doesn't appear to be interested in winning or in his brothers losing. He is only interested in fulfilling God's plan for his family's survival.

As Joseph's brothers arrive in Egypt looking for food, it appears that Joseph is plotting some elaborate "I'll get even with you!" scheme. He accuses them of being spies. He holds them prisoners. He insists they travel back home and bring their youngest brother, Benjamin, to him as proof that they are not lying. He plants their silver coins in their sacks and plants his silver cup in Benjamin's sack, almost giving them a heart attack over the situation. What kind of game was Joseph playing? Was he trying to even the score? I don't think so.

I believe Joseph's actions were a test of his brothers' character; he wanted to see if they realized their own guilt. He was deeply moved in the presence of his brothers on more than one occasion (Genesis 42:24; 43:30; 45:1–2),

COMPLETELY LOVED BY...OUR SLATE CLEANER

and I believe he had already forgiven them for the evil they had done and was eager to restore their relationship.

Consider his words of forgiveness and encouragement to his brothers:

> Don't be angry with yourselves that you did this to me, for *God did it. He sent me here* ahead of you to preserve your lives.... *God has sent me here* to keep you and your families alive so that you will become a great nation. Yes, it was *God who sent me here*, not you! And *he has made me a counselor to Pharaoh*—manager of his entire household and ruler over all Egypt.
>
> Hurry, return to my father and tell him, "This is what your son Joseph says: *God has made me master over all the land of Egypt.* Come down to me right away!" (Genesis 45:5–9)

Joseph wasn't interested in revenge, but rather in repentance and restoration. But how could he wipe their slate clean? The answer is found in Joseph's father's words to his brothers in Genesis 43:14, "May *God Almighty give you mercy* as you go before the man, that he might release Simeon and return Benjamin."

We can't manufacture such mercy in our human strength. God sowed mercy in Joseph's heart, and He can do the same in yours. Regardless of who has hurt you—a sibling who mistreated you, a parent who abused you, a friend who betrayed you, a spouse who has neglected you—you can choose, with God's help, to offer mercy instead of punishment. By refusing to keep score, you win in the long run.

Also remember that far beyond your present sufferings lies a sovereign plan lovingly designed by your heavenly Bridegroom, a plan "for good and not for disaster, to give you a future and a hope" (Jeremiah 29:11). As that plan unfolds, instead of keeping score against those who offend you, what can you do with your sufferings? Exactly what Paul encouraged the Romans to do: "*Rejoice* in our sufferings, because we know that suffering produces perseverance; perseverance, character; and character, hope" (Romans 5:3–4, NIV).

So girlfriend, rejoice in your sufferings, embrace perseverance, character, and hope as gifts from God, and with His help, wipe those slates clean!

HOLDING HIS HAND

Are there people whose sins I continue to count against them? Who and why?

_____

_____

_____

What good does it do me to keep score? Does harboring resentment in my heart play into God's ultimate plan for my life? Why or why not?

_____

_____

_____

How am I a stronger person because of the wrongs others have committed against me? Can I give thanks for the spiritual growth that has occurred as a result? If so, how?

_____

_____

_____

> _Lord Jesus,_
>
> _You are the ultimate example of how not to keep score! You were absolutely perfect and completely without sin, yet You chose to take on all of our sins so that we could be reconciled to our Holy Father. Oh, how we owe You such a debt of gratitude! Help us to show it by following Your example and freely extending forgiveness to others as well._

COMPLETELY
Loved BY...

OUR LEADERSHIP TRAINER

Daily reading: Genesis 39–41

Key passage: Joseph's suggestions were well received by Pharaoh and his advisers. As they discussed who should be appointed for the job, Pharaoh said, "Who could do it better than Joseph? For he is a man who is obviously filled with the spirit of God." (Genesis 41:37–38)

Long before Stephen Covey developed *The Seven Habits of Highly Effective People*, before Zig Ziglar's *See You at the Top* made it to the top of the best-seller list, and prior to Dale Carnegie teaching us *How to Win Friends and Influence People*, there existed an entirely different kind of leadership training. It was called God's Leadership School of Hard Knocks, and Joseph earned a doctoral degree during his thirteen-year tenure there.

Let's pick up the story after Joseph becomes a slave in Potiphar's house. Even though he's being held captive, things seem to be going well. Potiphar has put Joseph completely in charge because he recognizes that the Lord's favor is all over the young man. But God isn't the only one who favors Joseph. Potiphar's wife also takes a liking to the handsome young man and makes him the target of her lustful desires. Fortunately, Joseph has the integrity to refuse, even running away when necessary. His rejection embarrasses and angers her, so she tells her husband that Joseph tried to rape her. Not good. So long, Potiphar's house. Hello, prison cell.

Favor has followed Joseph from the pit his brothers tossed him into, to the Egyptian palace, and now from the palace to the prison. Within a short time Joseph is placed in leadership once again, although he's still a prisoner. The warden puts him in charge of all the other prisoners, and the Lord grants him great success there as well. One day he interprets dreams for two of Pharaoh's imprisoned servants. According to their dreams, Joseph predicts that the baker will soon die and the cupbearer will live. He then beseeches the cupbearer, "Hey, when you are released and restored to your position, don't forget about me! I don't belong here. I've been wrongly enslaved as well as wrongly accused. Mention me to Pharaoh, okay?"

But the cupbearer forgets, that is, until the God-ordained time arrives for Joseph to have his moment in Pharaoh's spotlight. Pharaoh is troubled by two dreams, and the cupbearer suggests that perhaps Joseph can explain them. Indeed he can, but Joseph is careful to mention that the interpretation comes from God, not from himself. Not only does he explain the dream, he also suggests a plan for careful administration during the next seven years of plenty, so that there will be food to fall back on during the ensuing seven years of famine. Surely a surprise to Joseph, Pharaoh replies, "Great! You've got the job! Welcome to the leadership team! Here's your ring and a robe, your gold chain and your chariot...oh, and here's a wife, too!"

Over a thirteen-year period, Joseph goes from the pit to the palace, then to the prison, and now back to the palace again, not as a slave, but as one of the mightiest rulers in the land. While we may be tempted to think that the story is about Joseph's success, we can't lose sight of the bigger picture. It's really about God's faithfulness to His promises to the Israelites, for how can the descendants of Abraham, Isaac, and Jacob become as numerous as the stars if they all starve to death in a great famine? Not only is Joseph's leadership a fulfillment of God's promises, it's also a fulfillment of Joseph's dreams as his brothers come and bow down before him in hopes of finding both favor and food.

But why couldn't Joseph have been exalted before his brothers sold him into slavery? Why did he have to suffer for thirteen years before coming into the position of leadership at the age of thirty? It was all God's timing. Because things happened as they did, Joseph learned the Egyptian customs and gained business administration experience. Due to the way he was trained, Joseph didn't become a pompous, prideful, oppressive leader like many others. He had learned to patiently bear the burdens of others because he had walked in their shoes—the poor, the enslaved, the foreigners, the imprisoned. He had sympathy for the plight of people, which made him a great servant leader.

Quite often, suffering fashions the best leaders. Not only do we see this in Joseph's case, but also in Jesus'. Consider the following verses from Hebrews:

- "Through the suffering of Jesus, God made him a perfect leader, one fit to bring them into their salvation" (Hebrews 2:10).
- "So even though Jesus was God's Son, he learned obedience from the things he suffered. In this way, God qualified him as a perfect High Priest, and he became the source of eternal salvation for all those who obey him" (Hebrews 5:8–9).
- "[Jesus] was willing to die a shameful death on the cross because of the joy he knew would be his afterward. Now he is seated in the place of highest honor beside God's throne in heaven. Think about all he endured when sinful people did such terrible things to him, so that you don't become weary and give up" (Hebrews 12:2–3).

Jesus' sufferings made him obedient to His Father, able to delay gratification, and a perfect leader to show us how to live.

As with both Jesus and Joseph, we sometimes suffer for no other reason than our faithfulness to God. However, keep in mind that the way we respond to suffering either qualifies us or disqualifies us for leadership. Rather than wasting our emotional energy on pitying ourselves, we can exercise our God-given power to make the best of every situation. We can humbly reach out to help others, regardless of how low on the totem pole we may be. We can trust that no matter how dark things seem, as long as we are holding on to our heavenly Bridegroom, He'll eventually lead us into the light. As in Joseph's case, the darkest hour often precedes the most glorious dawn.

So when you are experiencing difficulties in life, don't focus as much on your circumstances as on your Savior. Prayerfully ask the Lord how you can respond to your suffering in a way that will prepare you for any leadership role He has in mind for you.

HOLDING HIS HAND

What dark hours have you faced in life? Could it be that you have been a student in God's Leadership School of Hard Knocks?

_____

_____

_____

In your own words, describe how one can turn pain into power. What would be the benefits of doing such a thing?

_____

_____

_____

What things might your past pain equip you to do in leading others toward a better life for themselves?

_____

_____

_____

> _Lover of our Souls,_
>
> _Thank You for Your willingness to suffer for our sake, for You are truly the best leader imaginable. Teach me how to submit to whatever suffering this life brings, trusting that You have a purpose and a plan for it. Help me recognize the ways in which You are leading me to reach out to others as a result of my experiences, for I know You can ultimately use my suffering for my good, the good of others, and for Your glory._

COMPLETELY

Loved BY...

OUR DIVINE DEFENDER

Daily reading: Job 1:1–2:10; 42:10–17

Key passage: So the LORD blessed Job in the second half of his life even more than in the beginning. For now he had fourteen thousand sheep, six thousand camels, one thousand teams of oxen, and one thousand female donkeys. He also gave Job seven more sons and three more daughters.... Job lived 140 years after that, living to see four generations of his children and grandchildren. (Job 42:12–13, 16)

My husband and I watched a DVD recently, and after the first half, I had to speak up. "I hate this movie!" I declared. But the friend who loaned it to us had actually warned, "You may not like the story line until you see how it ends, but stick with it. It's worth it. Just pay close attention at the beginning." She was right. By the time the movie was over, I thought I'd actually like to watch it a second time. Knowing that it all ended on such a happy note, I figured I could watch the first part again with a completely different frame of mind.

Such is the case with the book of Job. As the story opens, we have this gut-wrenching feeling of *Why?* Why would You allow these terrible things to happen to Your servant, God? It doesn't seem fair at all! I don't like this story! But by the time we get to the last chapter, we realize that there's a very happy ending, as Job proves his honor and integrity and is blessed twice as much as before.

If we are to understand the part that our heavenly Bridegroom plays in this saga, we must pay attention to what goes on at the beginning. Reading the dialogue between Satan and God leads us to realize that this book isn't really about Job and his suffering. It is about God's divine defense of Job's character when Satan accuses him of being a fair-weather follower. "Take away everything he has, and he will surely curse you to your face!" Satan insists (Job 1:11). Job proves Satan wrong, so Satan ups the ante. "But take away his health, and he will surely curse you to your face!" (Job 2:5). The real attack is on God through Job, and the only way to prove Satan wrong is through Job as well. God allows such intense suffering in Job's life to prove His point to the accuser—that Job's love for God is based on who God is, not on what Job has or how he feels.

Viewed with this frame of mind, the story reads quite differently than perhaps we've understood it before. When it is time to put Satan in his place, Job is God's first-round draft pick. What an honor! God knows Job's love is real, and He doesn't allow Satan to bring more trouble into Job's life than he can handle—just enough to prove Satan wrong. God defends Job's integrity, and Job ultimately appears to be a spiritual hero rather than a victim. We can also rest assured that God knows our character, and He will protect us from Satan's schemes as well. Just as Job didn't receive more distress than he could withstand, neither will we because of God's supernatural defense.

Of course, Job had no idea why he was suffering such tragedies, but his faith in God's goodness never wavered. After learning about the loss of his cattle, sheep, camels, and even his sons and daughters, Job actually worships God and says, "Naked I came from my mother's womb, and naked I will depart. The LORD gave and the LORD has taken away; may the name of the LORD be praised" (Job 1:21, NIV). Even after his body is stricken with disease and his wife asks, "Are you still holding on to your integrity? Curse God and die!" Job replies, "You are talking like a foolish woman. Shall we accept good from God, and not trouble?" (Job 2:9–10, NIV). While we know the full story, remember that Job knew absolutely nothing of the conversation between God and Satan. His worshipful actions were a natural response to his confidence in God's goodness, not a fake act just so God could win the bet.

As difficult as this testing was, we would expect that Job would eventually question, challenge, and wrestle with God, swaying back and forth from trembling to trusting. While Job does struggle with his tragic circumstances, Satan's ultimate goal is never accomplished. When he tries to manipulate Job into cursing God, Job praises God instead. I can just imagine Satan turning around and slinking away with his tail between his legs, knowing he has been clearly beaten. I can also picture God beaming proudly and saying, "Yep, that's my boy!" as Job's trust in Him remains rock solid.

This was certainly a test that none of us hopes to take. But the book of Job reminds us that when we are frail and fearful due to adverse circumstances, God is our divine defender. He will stand up to Satan before our burdens become too heavy for us to bear. Regardless of physical ailments, mental distress, emotional turmoil, or spiritual testing, we can choose to rest securely in God's goodness, not just some of the time, but all of the time.

HOLDING HIS HAND

In what ways am I suffering during this season of my life? Could there be a divine reason behind it that I simply can't understand on this side of heaven? Can I choose to praise God anyway?

_____

_____

_____

What has today's reading taught me about my Divine Defender? Can I trust in His goodness regardless of my circumstances? Why or why not?

_____

_____

If God wanted to put Satan in his place today, would I be a first-round draft pick to accomplish the task? Why or why not?

_____

_____

_____

Most Holy God,

We acknowledge that we have a very limited understanding of why bad things happen to good people, but we trust in Your never-ending goodness, Lord. While we never want to be tested the way Job was, may every tragedy we ever experience in life still ultimately lead us to bless Your name, for You are worthy of our radical praise regardless of our circumstances. In Your Son's precious name. Amen.

COMPLETELY
Loved BY...

OUR EXTRAVAGANT LOVER

Daily reading: Hosea 1–3

Key passage: "But then I will win her back once again. I will lead her out into the desert and speak tenderly to her there. I will return her vineyards to her and transform the Valley of Trouble into a gateway of hope. She will give herself to me there, as she did long ago when she was young, when I freed her from her captivity in Egypt.

"In that coming day," says the LORD, "you will call me 'my husband' instead of 'my master.'... I will make you my wife forever, showing you righteousness and justice, unfailing love and compassion. I will be faithful to you and make you mine, and you will finally know me as LORD." (Hosea 2:14–16, 19–20)

During the first several months of our dating relationship, I hesitated to give Greg Ethridge my whole heart. Why? Because he was such a good guy. It's not that I wanted to give my heart to a bad guy; it's that I felt unworthy of his love. Greg had never rebelled against God or his parents. He had never fallen away from church. He had never engaged in premarital sex. I, on the other hand, had done all those things and was dragging around a boatload of guilt and shame as a result.

One night I tried to warn Greg about what he was getting himself into by considering marriage with a girl like me, thinking that I owed him a free jump-ship pass from our relationship. Surely a "good guy" like Greg couldn't possibly want a "bad girl" like me. Imagine my relief when he responded, "Shannon, your past makes absolutely no difference. I love you for who you are today and who God made you to be, and I want to help you become that woman."

One of the biggest hindrances that keeps us from enjoying a more intimate relationship with our heavenly Bridegroom is the same feeling—that such a good God couldn't possibly love such a not-so-good person. But as these passages from the book of Hosea vividly illustrate, God can forgive the most grievous of sins because of His extravagant love. Can you imagine the look in His eyes and the tone in His voice as God says of Israel, "I will win her back once again.… Speak tenderly to her.… She will give herself to me.… [She] will call me 'my husband'" (Hosea 2:14–16). He obviously misses His beloved Israel since she has turned away, and He has every intention of avidly pursuing her and stealing her heart away from her other lovers (or "Baals") so that she can be with the One to whom she truly belongs.

Further in this passage of Scripture, God is no longer speaking of his bride in third-person (referring to "her" as if she is not present). He begins speaking to her directly, and I believe He is also speaking the same words to you today:

> I will make you my wife forever, showing you righteousness and justice, unfailing love and compassion. I will be faithful to you and make you mine, and you will finally know me as LORD. (Hosea 2:19–20)

Do those words inspire you to abandon your fears of rejection and surrender your whole heart to your heavenly Bridegroom? I hope so, because the Creator is eagerly courting you, girlfriend, and He wants to usher you all the way to the altar. He wants you to commit yourself wholeheartedly to Him as His spiritual bride and to remain committed to Him forever.

He promises to be faithful to you, even if you are unfaithful to Him. His love for you is unconditional. He will never turn His back on you, will never forsake you, wouldn't dream of slamming the door and driving away, or ripping your heart out and stomping on it. God is different from any lover you have ever had or anyone who has ever given up on you. Most people have their limits as to how much they can take in a relationship. Not God. He loves you without limits, and He wants you to love Him without limits as well.

But one thing He absolutely will not do is force you to love Him. He doesn't *require* your love—He longs to *inspire* it. He has given you free will, because love isn't love if it is demanded. He wants to woo you to the altar with the promise of His lavish love and tender care. He longs to convince you that your sin—past, present, or future—does not flaw His perfect love for you in any way.

So how do you feel about the courtship you've experienced with your Creator over the past thirty days? What is your response to His extraordinary proposal to move to an even deeper level of intimacy with Him? Are you ready to allow Him to clothe you in white so that you can live a pure life in a fallen world (the theme of our next devotional in the series, *Completely Forgiven*)?

Are you committed to loving Jesus without limits, to becoming completely His? Are you eager to embrace your role as the beloved bride of Christ? Do you long to bask in His extravagant love forever and ever?

If so, won't you join me in joyfully responding to our extravagant Lover: *"I do!"*

HOLDING HIS HAND

Why does God refuse to force us into loving Him in return?

_____

_____

_____

Do I believe with all my heart that God is pursuing me as His bride regardless of my past? What proof do I have for what I believe?

_____

_____

Do I question the level of commitment that my heavenly Bridegroom has for me? Why or why not?

_____

_____

_____

Do I question my own level of commitment to Him? Why or why not?

_____

_____

_____

Creator God,

How can Your love for us be so pure and so passionate when we are such fallen creatures?

Thank You for not holding our past against us and for desiring an intimate relationship with us in spite of how we have been unfaithful to You. Continue to woo us with Your extravagant love and give us hearts to love You extravagantly as well.

Are You Ready to Take Another Step Closer?

*Y*ou've been diving deep into God's love letter to you for the past thirty days. You've been pursuing a more intimate walk with Him. You've been holding His hand, considering the wonder of His character and sovereignty, and meditating on what impact this intimate knowledge can have on your life. I hope you've caught your own personal glimpses of God and you recognize that He loves you completely.

Are you ready to take another step closer to having the passionate relationship with God you've dared to dream of? If so, you are ready for the next devotional in the series:

Completely Forgiven: Responding to God's Transforming Grace

In *Completely Forgiven*, we'll shift our focus from God's romantic pursuit of us to His matchless mercies. Looking at various biblical characters, we'll come to recognize that God doesn't just tolerate sinners—He even uses them in powerful ways to accomplish His divine purposes. We'll hold His hand on a daily basis once again, searching our hearts for clues as to how we still need to respond to our heavenly Bridegroom in order to feel like the pure and spotless bride He sees us as.

If you've ever felt like you've exhausted God's mercies and that you are no longer acceptable to Him, think again. He is extending His arm of hope to you, longing for you to latch on and let Him usher you from the pit of despair into His palace of peace. Regardless of how stained your heart has been, He longs to clothe you in white and prepare you for the wedding supper of the Lamb.

If you are ready to respond to God's transforming grace, I'll meet you in the next devotional.

A Note from Shannon

Are you looking for a unique idea for a women's retreat? One that will provide an extraordinary experience for women of all ages, from all walks of life? One that will drive home the encouraging principles presented in this book about how we can fully embrace our role as the beloved bride of Christ?

Consider hosting a *Completely His* women's event! Using my four-session DVDs, the special ladies in your church, on your campus, or within your circle of friends will experience the joy of committing their "bridal love" to Jesus Christ, their heavenly Bridegroom.

Because a bride doesn't feel like a bride until she walks down the aisle, this event resembles a wedding ceremony in many ways—a wedding unlike any other you've ever attended, a wedding that will provide a sweet foretaste of the great wedding supper of the Lamb that is yet to come for all of us someday!

My ministry assistants and I have coordinated these events for the past several years for groups as small as ten and as large as four hundred. Here are some personal testimonies about what these events have meant to participants:

> I've frequently heard that I am the bride of Christ, but I never grasped
> the magnitude of what that meant. But when Shannon gave us an
> opportunity to attend this event and pledge our bridal love to Christ,
> it all became powerfully real to me. Now I host these events myself
> because I want other women to experience the love I've found in my
> Heavenly Bridegroom.
>
> —Lyn, age 52

> Tears of joy flowed freely as I walked down the aisle to unite my
> candle with Christ's. Even if I get married to a wonderful man some-

day, no wedding will ever compare to this experience—at least not until I attend the wedding supper of the Lamb when Jesus actually returns for me.

—Tracy, age 20

You have to experience this event to believe how meaningful and life transforming it really is! It's worth every ounce of effort to see women truly feel as if they are *Completely His!*

—Samantha, age 38

For more information, go to www.shannonethridge.com. There you will find plenty of creative ideas, DVDs, and other products, and downloadable forms to assist you in coordinating your own *Completely His* women's event.

NOTES

Day 3

1. From the Serenity Prayer, most often attributed to Reinhold Niebuhr, 1943.

Day 13

1. Kenneth L. Barker and John R. Kohlenberger III, *The Expositor's Bible Commentary*, Abridged Edition: Old Testament (Grand Rapids, MI: Zondervan, 1994), 223.

Day 18

1. John MacArthur, *The MacArthur Bible Commentary* (Nashville, TN: Thomas Nelson, 2005), 261.

Day 25

1. Kenneth L. Barker and John R. Kohlenberger III, *The Expositor's Bible Commentary*, Abridged Edition: Old Testament (Grand Rapids, MI: Zondervan, 1994), 411.

2. John MacArthur, *The MacArthur Bible Commentary* (Nashville, TN: Thomas Nelson, 2005), 331.

Day 26

1. Kenneth L. Barker and John R. Kohlenberger III, *The Expositor's Bible Commentary*, Abridged Edition: Old Testament (Grand Rapids, MI: Zondervan, 1994), 370.

Topical Index

Scripture Index

About the Author

SHANNON ETHRIDGE is the best-selling author of *Every Woman's Battle* and co-author of the award-winning *Every Young Woman's Battle,* both of which have remained on the best-seller list since their release and have been reprinted in seven different languages.

She's written ten other books, including *Preparing Your Daughter for Every Woman's Battle* and *Every Woman's Marriage.*

Previously a youth pastor and abstinence educator, Shannon has a master's degree in counseling and human relations from Liberty University, and she speaks regularly on the Teen Mania Ministries campus and in a variety of other church and college settings.

She lives in East Texas with her husband, Greg, and their two children, Erin and Matthew.

Visit her Web site at *www.shannonethridge.com.*